THE HERITAGE OF DUBUQUE

An Architectural View

by

Lawrence J. Sommer

illustrated by

Carl H. Johnson, Jr.

Limited Edition, October, 1975

Second Edition, November, 1975

Library of Congress catalog number 75-29909

Manufactured by Tel Graphics, East Dubuque, Illinois U.S.A.

THE HERITAGE OF DUBUQUE

An Architectural View

by

Lawrence J. Sommer

illustrated by

Carl H. Johnson, Jr.

sponsored by

The First National Bank of Dubuque

Proceeds from the sale of this book go to the
development of the Dubuque Five Flags Civic Center.

Dedicated to
The Preservation of Dubuque's Architectural Heritage

The Heritage of Dubuque Publication Committee

Rev. Norbert C. Barrett
Mary Alice Carroll
Daniel K. Dittemore
King Herr
Carl H. Johnson, Jr.
Marilyn Kempthorne
Gordon Kilgore
W. Frank McCaw
John M. McDonald
Helen Mercer
Jacqueline Merritt
Dennis H. Naughton
Wayne A. Norman
Dr. Walter Peterson
Edward G. Raap
Harvey Schmitt
Lawrence J. Sommer
Alan B. Spensley
Robert C. Wiederaenders

Preface

Cities are living things. They are born, live and die. Each has its own unique history and, like a person, a personality all its own. And as each person's character bears the stamp of past experience, so it is with cities. A city is an evolving thing, moulded by physical environment, social, technological and economic change.

It is in the architecture of a city that we see vestigial evidence of its past. And if we look at these tangible reminders of the past with sensitivity, we can recognize the change in American social expectations and cultural values which are represented in architectural forms.

Dubuque, perhaps more than any other city in Iowa, maintains the evidence of its past in the architecture of its neighborhoods, its businesses and industries.

In this book the reader is presented the evidence of the history of Dubuque as it is reflected in its architecture. There is the log house, the most elemental architectural expression of man's utilization of the natural environment; the almost mythological symbol of the American Frontier Experience. We are shown reminders of the youthful exuberance, the cultural charm and elegance, and the self-satisfaction which characterized Dubuque at certain moments in its past.

This book is more than a reminder of the Dubuque that was, and more than an explanation of the Dubuque that is. It is also an eloquent reminder that in our planning for the future evolution of this city we must take care to ensure that its unique character is preserved.

Americans have only recently recognized that the preservation of such tangible evidence of our historic patrimony is a significant element in the social and cultural environment. We now see that we are most comfortable in an environment which provides a sense of cultural depth and continuity as we experiment with new ideas. If the preservation of the remarkable variety of architectural forms which characterizes Dubuque has been fortuitous, this need not be the case in the future. By careful planning, future generations will share our delight in the heritage of this city. It will satisfy the human need for a familiar environment as the city changes to meet new needs.

Adrian D. Anderson,
State Historic Preservation Officer
Iowa City, Iowa
1975

Table of Contents

Introduction

Dubuque is Iowa's oldest city and the site of the first white settlement in the state. Located amid the rugged bluffs of the Upper Mississippi River, the "Key City of Iowa" can look back upon a rich heritage of lead mining, steamboating, railroading, lumbering and manufacturing. Dubuque has also been a center of education, religious training and the performing arts. Just as few cities its size can boast of such diversified economic enterprise, few can point with pride to three colleges and universities, three theological seminaries, several religious orders and a history of theater that dates to its first decade of existence. Dubuque's contributions to Iowa history include more "firsts" than any other community in the state. The first settlement, first house, first school, first church, first college, first sawmill and first theater are just a few of Dubuque's historical achievements that rank at the top of any such listing for Iowa communities.

Most places with an historical legacy as rich and varied as Dubuque's also possess a visual and architectural heritage worthy of that legacy. Dubuque is no exception, for the men and women with the courage to develop her resources and economy also had the imagination to erect houses, churches, schools and other buildings that reflect determination and pride in their accomplishments.

Like most other American cities, Dubuque's unique architectural heritage has largely been ignored until recent years. Many of the city's finest buildings have been lost, and many more have been allowed to deteriorate to the point where the cost of renovating or maintaining them may be too high to justify keeping them. It is difficult to change the effects of a half-century of neglect in some instances, but fortunately the past few years have seen a resurgence of interest, both public and private, in the preservation of Dubuque's old buildings. As a result of this increased awareness and interest in the city's historical architecture *The Heritage of Dubuque; An Architectural View* was proposed. The concept of the book grew from private interest in a number of local historic preservation opportunities and the resultant city-sponsored preliminary survey of historical and architecturally significant structures that included over five hundred separate buildings and classified them into four categories of relative importance to the city.

Utilizing this survey, *The Heritage of Dubuque; An Architectural View* outlines and describes the city's architectural development during the period from 1830-1930. This century of Dubuque architecture is divided into three broad segments that parallel both the Key City's historical progress and the changing trends of nineteenth and twentieth century American architecture. When reading this book, it is important to view the different buildings discussed as representative examples of various stylistic or construction developments related to Dubuque's architectural heritage. There are many other significant structures in Dubuque, to be sure, but time and space limitations prevent their inclusion. For the same reasons it is not possible to provide detailed histories and descriptions of all the buildings that are included. The choice of examples is based upon the citywide preservation planning survey previously referred to and upon the need to illustrate certain aspects of a particular architectural development.

Dubuque, The Key City

Dubuque, The Key City

Strategically situated on the Upper Mississippi almost midway between Saint Louis and Saint Paul, Dubuque became known as "the Key City of Iowa." As early as 1858 the Dubuque *Express and Herald* noted:

> We are at the most important point on the Upper Mississippi, a point which has given our city the sobriquet of "Key City." She commands, as the key, the whole of Northeastern Iowa and Southern Minnesota. . . . we might go on to show, in addition to her commercial advantages, that Dubuque must necessarily become, in time, a great manufacturing point, from the fact that her advantages for receiving lumber are equal to any other city in the entire West . . .[1]

Within ten years Dubuque's lumber mills were being supplied by rafts of logs from the pineries of Wisconsin and Minnesota. Many other industries also developed, making present-day Dubuque one of the most important manufacturing centers of Iowa.

In 1673 Louis Joliet and Father Jacques Marquette traveled downriver past the site of Dubuque, and became the first white men to explore the area. They came from Canada by way of the Great Lakes and the Wisconsin River. For nearly a century the vast region they explored was claimed by the French.

During the first half of the eighteenth century the frontiers of English settlement gradually moved westward. As the Indian lands were invaded, a series of frontier skirmishes between the French and English occurred beginning in 1754. In North America these battles were known as the French and Indian War and were part of a wider European conflict known as the Seven Years War. Under the terms of the Treaty of Paris that ended the conflict in 1763, the victorious British won Canada and all other French-held territory east of the Mississippi. For help received during the war, France gave Spain New Orleans and all of her land west of the Mississippi including what was later to be Dubuque.

The Spanish held claim to the west bank of the Mississippi River from 1763 until 1800 when it was ceded back to France under terms of a secret treaty with Napoleon. During this period the American Revolution occurred, which lasted from 1775 to 1783. In 1780, British soldiers even attacked settlements along the Upper Mississippi capturing the lead mines near Dubuque. During this British incursion, Jean Marie Cardinal, who had been mining at Dubuque as early as 1769, escaped to warn Saint Louis, and was killed while defending that city. The British were defeated there, but the Revolutionary War dragged on until 1783 when the Peace of Paris was signed giving the United States all the lands south of Canada and as far west as the Mississippi River. Historians say that this boundary might well have been at the Allegheny Mountains had it not been for Cardinal's warning and the defeat of the British at Saint Louis. In 1803 Napeoleon sold Louisiana to the United States and thus the region that encompasses present-day Dubuque became American.

Even as the Peace of Paris was being concluded in 1783 a French Canadian named Julien Dubuque was traveling to Prairie du Chien. During the next few years he made several visits to a Fox Indian village located near the mouth of Catfish Creek. He became a trusted friend of the tribe and, in 1788, received permission to work the nearby lead mines. His grant extended for twenty-one miles along the west bank of the Mississippi and was officially approved by the Spanish Governor at New Orleans in 1796. With help from his Indian friends Dubuque worked his "Mines of Spain" and bartered furs until his death in 1810. Each fall he took the lead and furs downriver to Saint Louis where he wintered and made preparations for the next season. A monument overlooking the mouth of Catfish Creek and the site of the Fox village Dubuque first visited marks the final resting place of this French entrepreneur who gave his name to the present city.

In the years that followed Julien Dubuque's death, the government, honoring a treaty with the Fox Indians, prevented any other white men from working the "Mines of Spain." Only once, in 1830, while the Indians were away, did miners cross the Mississippi for more than a brief period. They were driven out when the Fox returned.

The Dubuque region was finally thrown open for permanent settlement on June 1, 1833 as stated in the terms of the Black Hawk treaty. Hundreds of people, including many future Dubuque notables, crossed the river to engage in lead mining and other frontier enterprises. That same year Dubuque was established. The first raft of lumber from Wisconsin reached Dubuque in November, 1833, enabling a few crude houses to be built before winter set in, but most of the first settlers lived in log cabins hastily built of timber hewed from nearby forests.

By 1834 the lead mines were well established and a smelter was erected near the mouth of Catfish Creek. The Methodists built the first church in Iowa, a log cabin located in what is now Washington Park. A year later Father Samuel Mazzuchelli designed a stone church building that became the first Saint Raphael's Church. George Wallace Jones of Sinsinawa was elected territorial delegate to the United States Congress representing the Michigan Territory of which Iowa was then a part and with his help Iowa was included in the newly-formed Wisconsin Territory in 1836. The village of Dubuque was incorporated by the territorial legislature of Wisconsin in 1837. The *DuBuque Visitor*, the first newspaper north of Saint Louis and west of the Mississippi, was published in 1836. Before the end of the decade the oldest college in Iowa, known today as Loras College, was founded at Dubuque.

During the 1840's the lead trade prospered to the point where the annual value of lead sent from the Galena-Dubuque region was more than double that of the Missouri River fur trade and the traffic on the Santa Fe Trail. This was the peak of the lead mining era, however, and Dubuque was also becoming a steamboating, flour milling and lumbering center.

By 1850 the city's mixed population of Germans, Irish and English was well established, and a period of prosperity set in that lasted until the Civil War. Steamboat and railroad transportation improved, a few local fortunes were made and several landmark buildings of Dubuque were constructed. Among the significant local buildings built during the 1850's were the city hall, county jail, shot tower, Dubuque Female College, Mathias Ham house, Edward Langworthy octagon house, and Cathedral of Saint Raphael.

Between 1850 and 1860 Dubuque's population increased from 3,100 to 13,000. Gas street lights were installed, a steam ferry to Illinois began operation and telegraph lines reached the city. There were seven daily newspapers by decade's end. It was during this period that Dubuque gained its nickname "Key City."

The Civil War temporarily interrupted the wild growth of the previous ten years. Dubuque was a jumping off point for many troops being transported south, including two local companies — the Governor's Greys and the Jackson Guards. Lead mining had decreased by this time, but Dubuque's economy weathered the war reasonably well. Dubuque matured somewhat during the 1860's and was no longer the frontier mining town in which travelers shared beds at the few inns only to be kept awake by noisy miners in the barroom.[2] By 1865 Dubuque was recognized as a regional financial center, and the city's oldest continuously-operating bank, the First National, was established.

Between 1865 and 1870 a new era of rapid growth began. A railway bridge across the Mississippi was built, and additional rail connections to other parts of Iowa and the West were completed. Meat packing, brewing and wagon building industries developed.

Dubuque's post Civil War economic growth continued at a high rate throughout the 1870's and 1880's. It was during these years that sawmilling and woodworking became important local industries. The local demand for logs from Wisconsin and Minnesota became so great that it could hardly be met by the rafters who brought the logs downriver. The huge Standard Lumber Company was only one of many important Dubuque woodworking firms. Others, including Farley and Loetscher, and Carr, Ryder and Adams, were among the world's largest producers of doors, windows, cabinets and similar products. A local furniture industry that attracted many skilled German craftsmen also developed. Started in 1867 as the Dubuque Cabinet Makers Association, it prospered as the demand for new furniture grew. Their original factory was located at Tenth and White in a structure now used by the Rhomberg Fur Company. The city's role as a leading woodworking center has continued up to the present with many of the manufacturing firms that were organized after the Civil War still in business.

Many of Dubuque's educational and religious institutions were also established during the last half of the nineteenth century. Theater and other cultural opportunities were increased. Many civic improvements were made including the formation of the Dubuque Street Railway Company and the establishment of gas, water and electric utilities.

The late nineteenth century was the time in which much of Dubuque's unique architectural character was created. Most of the remaining Main Street and Central Avenue commercial structures, many houses along the bluffs and entire neighborhoods in the "North End" and "Point" areas were erected between the Civil War and the turn of the century. An 1897 description of Dubuque noted:

> The principal portion of the incorporation is located on table lands, gently sloping from high bluffs to the banks of the river, affording a fine perspective and excellent drainage, while the higher ranges furnish commanding sites for numerous institutions of learning and thousands of palatial residences, interspersed with handsome cottages and vine-clad homes of less pretentious appearance . . .[3]

In 1900 Dubuque's population was 36,297, and the city embarked upon a period of stability that lasted until World War II. Between 1900 and 1940 the total population increased by only two-thirds as much as it did in the single decade between 1850 and 1860. By the beginning of the twentieth century nearly all the great steamboat companies had gone out of business. Lumber rafting disappeared as the white pine logging industry moved into northeastern Minnesota, and the vast timber resources of the Pacific Northwest were opened. Dubuque continued to be an important manufacturing center, however, and, for a time, even automobiles were built at the Adams-Farwell factory. Major civic improvements included the development of Eagle Point Park. The heyday of Dubuque theater occurred during this period with the Grand Opera House, Orpheum and other theaters attracting the nation's top entertainers. Horse racing was popular at Nutwood Park, and Union Park also flourished as an amusement and family outing center.

The city's centennial in 1933, the close of the period this book deals with, was celebrated by a giant festival. It was highlighted by the attendance of two great-grand-nieces of Julien Dubuque.

NOTES ON THE C. P. FERRING PAINTINGS

The seven color plates that accompany this brief overview of Dubuque's historical development were painted by Cyril P. Ferring, a native of Dubuque and a distinguished artist. Ferring was commissioned in 1964 to paint the seven panels for the lower lobby of the First National Bank Building.

Ferring's panels commemorate the bank's century of operation and service to Dubuque. They also provide a colorful panorama of local history from the time of Julien Dubuque to the present. The seven panels are made from select species of various native hardwoods and hang chronologically along a backdrop of the Mississippi River. The original of the river backdrop is an old river chart by a traveling artist who made notes and sketches while paddling along the river. Later, these rough sketches were enlarged and painted on lengths of canvas that were twelve feet high and several hundred feet long. These "panoramas", as they were called, were slowly unrolled while a narrator recounted the scenic wonders of the Mississippi River Valley to an attentive audience.

Julien Dubuque and the Mines of Spain

Although preceded through the region by Father Marquette and Louis Joliet, Julien Dubuque, the French Canadian trader, was one of the first white men to live at the site of present-day Dubuque.

This painting is on a panel of hard maple, one of the area's most beautiful trees. Its subject matter includes the following:

Coats of arms of New France and Spain
Sac and Fox Indians
Julien Dubuque dressed as a French Canadian voyageur
The bluff on which Dubuque is now buried
A voyageur companion of Julien Dubuque
The Fox Indian village at the mouth of Catfish Creek
Early mining implements and scenes of mining activity

The Beginning of Settlement and Growth

Once the Fox Indian lands were opened for settlement in 1833, several hundred persons moved across the river from Illinois and Wisconsin to stake out their mining claims, build their cabins and establish the foundations for Dubuque's future growth.

The second panel is painted on white elm, a very symmetrical and graceful tree. The subject matter includes:

White elm trees
Ducks, grouse, wild turkey, jackrabbits: all important food sources
The Newman cabin, now at the Mathias Ham Museum
Keelboats, flatboats and river raft
Mining implements and activities
Early rivermen and miners
Miscellaneous settlers' goods and stock

Steamboats, Rafts and Sawmills

With the expansion of the Midwest the need for building materials increased. Dubuque became an important location for the processing of wood products cut from logs rafted downstream from the "northwoods" of Wisconsin and Minnesota.

Ferring painted this panel on black cherry, a valuable cabinet making wood. The scene includes:

Black cherry trees, leaves and berries
Great horned owl, ducks, blue heron, falcon and whooping cranes
Logging, rafting and sawmilling scenes

Hammers, Anvils, Steam and Wheels

The decade of the 1850's was a period of rapid growth. More than five hundred buildings were erected in a single year, gas street lights were installed and the local population tripled.

This painting is on a panel of butternut, a tree commonly found both along stream banks and in open woods. Its subject matter includes:

Various steamboats and other river craft
Agricultural activity and implements
Immigrant wagon waiting to cross the river on a ferry
Fishermen and river fish
Early railroading scenes

Era of Decision, The Civil War

The year 1864 marked the founding of Dubuque's First National Bank. It also marked a nation torn by Civil War, economic uncertainty verging on chaos, and the completion of the Illinois Central railway as far west as Dunleith, just across the river from Dubuque.

This panel is painted on white oak, favored for building and furniture making in America since colonial times. Among the subjects included in the painting are:

The old Washington Park Gazebo
Civil War soldiers and firearms
First Town Clock
City Hall
Old Dubuque County Court House
Old Custom House and Post Office

Dubuque at the Turn of the Century

Ferring painted this panel on red oak, another important source of lumber. The subjects illustrated include:

First railroad bridge across river
The present Town Clock
Red oak tree leaves and acorns
Julien Dubuque's monument
Adams-Farwell automobile made in Dubuque
Miscellaneous Dubuque scenes and activity including bicycling, local residents and houses
Harness racing at Nutwood Park
The Dubuque County Court House
Excursion steamboat
A Cooper wagon box and Connolly carriage
Electric lights, wall telephone, windmill and threshing machine

Dubuque in the Twentieth Century

Various aspects of the modern diversified city are illustrated in the last of the seven Ferring panels. It is painted on black walnut, the most valuable of local timber species. Among the scenes illustrated are:

The five flags that have flown over Dubuque
Dubuque churches
Dubuque schools and colleges
Local hospitals, homes and other buildings
Walnut leaves
Various aspects of trade, agriculture, manufacturing, transportation and other Dubuque economic endeavors
Family and home life

Lost Heritage

Landmarks That Have Disappeared

Lost Heritage

In 1932 when an old house was being demolished to make way for a new Central Avenue business, a newspaper account noted the event and quoted the demolition contractor as saying he "had wrecked many landmarks but had never before seen a building so strongly constructed."[1] The building he was tearing down was Dubuque's first octagon house. It had been standing since well before the Civil War and was built by a family named Eichorn. It had eight inch thick concrete walls reinforced at the corners with oak branches imbedded in the mortar. Such a solid structure could probably still be standing as are several other Dubuque buildings just as old and not as well built.

Old buildings, however, are not only torn down by wrecking crews. In Dubuque, as in other cities, there are many agents of destruction. Some buildings must be demolished because they become unsafe and cannot be repaired, but others are destroyed by fire, tornados and floods as well as by neglect, public apathy and the changing nature of cities themselves. No amount of preparation or foresight, of course, can prevent the sudden impact of a natural disaster, but the activities of man have destroyed most of the historic buildings the United States has lost.

The loss of landmark buildings through the processes of urban change has been evident in Dubuque from the time it was settled. At first, crude miners' shacks were scattered along the base of the bluffs and up the valleys. By 1850 a business district was centered around Main and Second Streets while the blocks we know today as the center of downtown were residential in character. After the Civil War, the business district moved northward along Main Street, and houses were built in large numbers above the bluffs overlooking the Mississippi. At the same time, new residential sections were created in the "North End" closer to many of the city's expanding industries. After a period of stability in the early twentieth century, rapid growth occurred during the 1950's and 1960's causing the subdivision of many farms that were formerly on the western outskirts of Dubuque. At the same time urban renewal was dramatically changing the appearance of what had been Dubuque's central business district for nearly a century.

During the 150 years of continual change in the urban scene literally hundreds of buildings were torn down. Among the losses were several of the most significant landmarks constructed in the city, representing an irreplaceable part of the heritage of Dubuque.

Because Dubuque's architectural heritage is so rich, the city has been able to afford the landmark losses that have occurred and yet maintain its unique character. The forgotten landmarks illustrated on the following pages should serve as reminders, however, that even an urban character and architecture as wonderful as Dubuque's is fragile and in danger of being lost altogether.

Many local residents will probably remember some of Dubuque's lost landmarks. They are from every period of the city's history and are representative of the full range of causes that destroy such structures. While the loss of some landmarks is inevitable and there are many buildings that are not really worth saving, the decision to tear down any old building should always be carefully made considering all the issues involved.

The Dubuque Town Clock

Probably the most spectacular landmark loss in Dubuque's history occurred on May 25, 1872 when the old town clock building collapsed. Three persons including an infant were killed. The Dubuque *Weekly Times* noted:

We record the most awful calamity which ever overtook the people of this city. At about 5 minutes past 5 o'clock Saturday afternoon, without a moment's warning, the town clock building on the west side of Main, between 8th and 9th Streets, occupied as a dry goods store by John Bell & Company, fell with a terrible

> crash, burying beneath the debris those who happened to be in the store at the moment and endangering the lives of two or three parties who were standing or passing on the street at the time.[2]

The old clock had been a Dubuque landmark since it was erected in 1865 at a cost of some $3,000. The idea of a town clock was first suggested in 1864 by Dr. Asa Horr. A year later the Dubuque Town Clock Company was formed by subscribers to erect and maintain a clock. The architect was William Longhurst of Chicago. Dubuque residents were proud of their town clock as contemporary accounts record that:

> Competent judges say it kept the best time of any clock in the United States, a fact admitted by watchmakers and adepts in time keeping, and largely due to the skillful superintendance of Dr. Horr.[3]

After the collapse of the old clock, a new one was designed by Dubuque architect Fridolin Heer. It was completed and put into operation April 17, 1873. Today, over a hundred years later, local residents still set their watches by this town clock.

The Wales Hotel

The Wales Hotel, located at Eighth and Bluff, where the *Telegraph Herald* Building now stands, was built in 1856 by Peter Lorimier. Known as the Lorimier House, it was operated as a boarding house until 1870. From 1870 until 1894 a relative of Lorimier's ran the Lorimier House as a hotel. Charles Wales purchased the building in 1894. He renamed it the Wales Hotel and operated it successfully until fire destroyed it in 1917.

The old Wales Hotel had 110 rooms, thirty-five baths, and the rates were $2.50 to $3.50 per day.

The Illinois Central Passenger Depot →

The rise of the automobile as America's chief mode of transportation after World War II resulted in virtual abandonment of railway passenger service and the closing of depots across the country. A few of the once proud depots have been converted to contemporary uses, but many others have been demolished. Dubuque's

Illinois Central passenger depot still stands below Jones Street but bears no resemblance to its original design. The tower, porches and upper story dormitory are gone. When passenger service ended, it was remodeled into a freight terminal.

Eleventh Street Elevator

The success of Dubuque's Fourth Street or Fenelon Place Elevator spurred the erection of a similar conveyance at Eleventh Street in 1887. Two years later an elaborate platform decorated with Chinese lanterns was built at the summit, and for many years the ride and view were popular with local residents. The Eleventh Street Elevator operated until about World War I when lack of patronage forced it out of business. It was demolished in 1929, but the route up the bluff is still plainly visible.

The Dubuque Custom House and Post Office

Construction of Dubuque's Custom House and Post Office began in 1857 but was interrupted by the nationwide panic and depression of that year and again by the Civil War so the building was not completed until 1866. It was located at the corner of Ninth and Locust. By the time it finally was completed, the cost was $175,000 or more than double the original estimate. Ely S. Parker, West Point graduate, colonel on the staff of U. S. Grant and designer of the post office at Galena, was the architect. Until the completion of Dubuque's new post office in 1934, it was one of the oldest post offices west of the Mississippi River.

Contemporary accounts of the construction noted that the design of the Dubuque Custom House "is all that could be desired to fill the requirements of strength, durability, commodiousness with the neat beauty yet rich simplicity unburdened by any excess of ornament."[4] The building was erected of cut limestone, some of which was reported to have come from the ruins of the Mormon Temple at Nauvoo, Illinois, destroyed after the Mormons left in 1846. The interior of the Custom House was finished with stucco walls, mahogany woodwork and ornamental iron that came from the firm of Stewart and Company, Wheeling, West Virginia.

Even before its completion, local interest in the project was high. The Dubuque *Times* commented on its construction in 1861:

> We shall have in return for the princely cost of this building an edifice as durable almost as our bluffs. The floor may have to be relaid every fifty years and the roof replaced centennially, but with these slight repairs it will otherwise attain as respectable an age as the oldest castle on the Rhine.[5]

The Dubuque Custom House and Post Office was torn down in 1947 to permit construction of the present Northwestern Bell Telephone Company building.

The James Langworthy House →

"Ridgemount" was built in 1849, and was considered to be the finest house along the Upper Mississippi River. It was located at James and Langworthy Streets and for many years was the scene of important local social affairs.

The house was built of brick manufactured in the Langworthy Brothers own brickyard. Its furnishings were purchased in New York, shipped through the Gulf of Mexico to New Orleans and up the Mississippi to Dubuque. Ninety-six years after its construction, the house was torn down in 1945 when the new Mercy Hospital was built.

James L. Langworthy and his brother, Lucius, came to this area from Galena in 1830. They mined lead for a short time before being removed by federal authorities because the land was not yet open to white settlers. They returned in 1833 to settle permanently. At the time Dubuque was chartered in 1836 the Langworthys owned all the land from Bluff Street to Alpine Street and from Dodge Street to University Avenue. They also owned large tracts of land in the vicinity of what is now Kaufmann Avenue.

The James Marsh Residence

This outstanding Italian Villa house was built in 1854 by James Marsh. Marsh's wife, Harriet, was the sister of the four Langworthy brothers.

Located at 1049 University Avenue, the house was to be Harriet Marsh's dream, but she died before it was completed. Despite this tragedy, Marsh completed the house as planned. It had eight fireplaces carved of carrara marble from the quarries of Pietro Santo near Rome, a walnut staircase and woodwork throughout that was carved by a Swiss craftsman brought to Dubuque specifically for the job. The house also had French window glass and mirrors, bronze chandeliers and a double front door of carved walnut.

After the Marshes the house was occupied by Mrs. Anna P. Slattery. In 1944 it was purchased by the Delbert Hayfords who lived in it until its sale and demolition to create a playground for Nativity School during the 1960's.

This house was the most elegantly furnished of all the Langworthy homes. For many years some of the most important furnishings from the Marsh house were in California. After prolonged negotiations, they are back in Dubuque and can be seen at the Mathias Ham Museum.

The Samuel Dixon House

Samuel Dixon came to Dubuque in 1837 and built this simple frame house at Tenth and Main in 1839. At that time the business district was confined along Main between First and Third Streets. Little is known of Dixon's background, but in 1839 he was elected to the Town Board of Trustees and in 1892 was elected to one term as Mayor.

Dixon's house had eight rooms and eight fireplaces, oak floors and a cherry staircase. Before it was torn down for a parking lot it had passed through several owners who maintained it with varying degrees of care.

The James A. Beach House

Dubuque businessman James A. Beach built this fine Italian Villa with its octagonal tower at 1183 Locust in 1873. It was torn down to permit construction of the present Masonic Temple. The firm of James Beach and Sons was incorporated in 1878 and became a prominent manufacturer of soap products during the 1880's. Their factory was located near Dodge and Locust.

The William Peabody House

The Peabody house was built during the late 1870's at 1428 Locust Street. It featured Italian marble fireplaces and beautifully carved woodwork. From 1906 until 1960 the house was used as a rectory for Saint John's Episcopal Church. It was torn down to provide parking space in 1964. Peabody came to Dubuque from Syracuse, New York in 1856 and established successful mercantile and wholesale liquor businesses. During the 1860's and 1870's his firm was located at Third and Main.

The Old Julien Hotel →

The first hotel at the corner of Second and Main was the Waples House built in 1844 by Peter Waples. In 1854 its name changed to the Julien House. Fire destroyed this hotel in 1889, but a year later a new building was completed. The 1890 Julien Hotel is the one illustrated here. It was the scene of many important events, and its register of prominent guests included John L. Sullivan, General U.S. Grant, Mark Twain and Buffalo Bill Cody. In 1913 the building was destroyed by fire. The present Julien Motor Inn now occupies the site.

Old Dubuque County Court House →

This massive brick structure was built in 1839 to house the offices of Dubuque County government. Both Samuel Wilkings and Joseph Ogilby were credited as being the architect, but apparently Wilkings drew the preliminary sketches (for a fee of $8.00) while Ogilby prepared the final drawings. The Langworthy brickyards furnished the brick, and it was reported that the builder used 244,518 bricks to complete the structure. In 1856 John F. Rague designed an addition that extended the original structure to the west. The old Dubuque County Court House was torn down in 1891 to permit construction of the present county government building.

The Milwaukee Railroad Shops →

In 1871 the Chicago, Milwaukee and Saint Paul Railroad established what were known as the Milwaukee Shops. They employed 2,000 workers and were the city's largest industry for many years. The shops were located south of Railroad Street near present day Maus Lake. When the railroad closed the shops, many buildings were demolished, but an engine round house and other remains can still be seen.

Western Brewery

The Western Brewery was located near the terminus of Hill Street. It was built in 1847 and consisted of a brewery, ice house, two residences, a beer hall and pagoda. It was operated by M. Tschirgi and J. Schwind and had a capacity of 300 barrels per week. They employed ten men. The Western Brewery went out of business sometime before 1900, and the buildings were torn down to allow new development. ↓

Tivoli Gardens →

The beer garden has been an integral part of Dubuque's social history for over one hundred years. Perhaps the best known of the local beer gardens that have existed throughout the years was the Tivoli. It was located in a grove of oak trees that originally extended along Central Avenue from Kaufmann to West 23rd Street and westerly as far as present-day Francis Street.

Kaufmann Avenue was originally known as Langworthy Hollow and was the location of the first lead strikes by Lucius and Edward Langworthy. West 23rd Street was originally Hart Street, the family name of the four Langworthy brothers' mother. Francis Street was originally spelled Frances Street after Lucius Langworthy's first wife, and Valeria Street is named after his second wife.

The Greek Revival frame house that became the focal point for the Tivoli Gardens was built by John Schaffner in 1851. The Gardens opened soon afterward with Schaffner as the first operator. They remained popular for nearly fifty years.

Although the oak grove was owned by the Langworthy family and was gradually subdivided, Schaffner's house passed through several owners and was not torn down until the 1930's.

Union Park

Union Park was owned by the Union Electric Company and was a center for amusements, picnicking, dancing, bowling, swimming and other attractions. The park was established in 1891 and operated until the increasing popularity of the automobile caused its demise in 1934. Streetcars ran to the park every ten minutes. Its ballroom was the largest in Iowa and often attracted 800 couples per night. In 1919 a flash flood roared through the park killing five persons.

After the flood the dance hall was moved and reconstructed as Melody Mill. The roller coaster was also torn down after several years of steadily declining business.

The Old Central Engine House

Located at Ninth and Iowa, the Central Engine House was constructed in 1892. The architect was T. T. Carkeek. The first and second floors housed the fire department, and the third was used as an armory. Dubuque's first motorized fire pumper, nicknamed Jumbo, was delivered in 1912, but the last horse drawn rig was not replaced until 1918. The old Central Engine House was demolished in October, 1970 as part of Dubuque's urban renewal program after its replacement by the new fire headquarters building.

Fort Rittenhouse

Fort Rittenhouse was never a fort but rather a house that was built in 1846 by Col. Rufus Rittenhouse, a pioneer Dubuque contractor and businessman. Because of its rugged Montrose Terrace site and splendid river view, the house became known locally as Fort Rittenhouse. Unlike many other landmarks, the building still stands but bears little resemblance to its original appearance because of modernization during the 1960's.

Turner Hall

→

Turner Hall was built in 1856 at the corner of Twelfth and Central. Sponsored by the Saengerbund and Krieger Verein societies, Turner Hall had a long history as a meeting and entertainment center, public grade school, Dubuque's first high school and Boys Club until it was torn down in 1935 so the site could be used as a playground for Prescott School. As demolition started during the autumn of 1935 a longtime neighborhood resident reported to the newspaper that the cornerstone would be found to contain some interesting papers and a bottle of good liquor.[6]

The Connelly-Nagle House →

This outstanding Queen Anne style house at 1637 Iowa Street was designed and built in 1893 by Thomas Connelly, a Dubuque businessman and carriage factory owner. At the time of its completion it was one of the finest homes in the city. Many hardwoods were used throughout including mahogany in the parlour and library, oak in the dining room, and sycamore, maple and butternut in the second floor bedrooms. Built of red Colorado sandstone, the Connelly House had many stained glass windows and was one of the few homes in Dubuque with a carriage step that enabled entrance from carriages without stepping on the ground. Another unusual feature was the air circulation system. The large opening under the porch was the intake for this ventilation system.

Dubuque businessman John J. Nagle bought the house from Connelly in 1921 and occupied it for many years. During the last decade the house stood vacant and neglected. It burned in January, 1973 and was condemned by the city. Rather than be demolished, however, the ruins were rebuilt into apartments. Although saved from total destruction, the building's inherent architectural qualities have been destroyed.

The John Emerson House

The John Emerson mansion was constructed during the 1870's at the location of what is now Wartburg Seminary. It was one of the most elaborate Italian Villa houses ever built in Dubuque. In 1881 a mortgage on the property was foreclosed by a New York bank. The property was bought by the Dubuque Board of Trade and given to Wartburg Seminary in 1888 as an inducement to return to Dubuque. An addition to the house was built, and it served as the seminary's home until construction of the present Wartburg buildings between 1914 and 1916.

The Bissell-Babbage-Andrew-McDonald House →

The Bissell-Babbage-Andrew-McDonald House was one of the earliest and most elaborate examples of Gothic Revival architecture in Iowa. Designed by John F. Rague, it led the way for Dubuque's "gingerbread" architecture of the post Civil War period.[7]

Frederick E. Bissell built the house in 1857 but the nationwide panic and depression of that year forced him to sell it to R. A. Babbage who in turn sold it to William Andrew. It occupied half a block on Eleventh Street between Locust and Bluff Streets. The A. Y. McDonald family occupied the house for nearly twenty years, longer than any other owner.

This exceptional structure was torn down to permit construction of the two Stout houses in the early 1890's. The two round windows seen in the gables are still in existence, having been moved to a house near Finley Hospital.

Washington Park Gazebo →

The gazebo in Washington Park was a downtown landmark for many years. Similar structures also stood in Jackson and Madison Parks. As so often happens, age and neglect took their toll and the quaint landmarks were finally torn down. The Washington Park gazebo may come back to life, however, as part of a major renovation scheme planned for 1976. It is scheduled for reconstruction as part of the park improvement.

The August A. Cooper Residence →

"Greystone" was built in 1888 by Dubuque wagon maker August A. Cooper. It had four floors and thirty-five rooms that were finished in cherry, mahogany, maple and other fine hardwoods. One of the finest Queen Anne houses ever built in Dubuque, "Greystone" was razed in 1956 to make room for the municipal parking lot at Fifth and Bluff.

Cooper came to Dubuque in 1848, worked as an apprentice and started his own wagon factory in 1850. By 1865 he employed over 150 persons and was producing 5,000 wagons per year. They were sold in twenty-seven states and territories. Cooper wagons were known for their rugged quality. Many of them were known to have crossed the continent without the need for repairs. His factory was the largest wagon works in Iowa.

Cooper also built two other family houses nearby. One was torn down in 1934 when the new Post Office was constructed, and the other, "Redstone" still stands at 504 Bluff Street.

Main Street

Many of Dubuque's Main Street commercial buildings were constructed during the 1870's and 1880's. They were similar in scale and architectural style giving an overall unity to the downtown streetscape. During recent years, however, much of this interesting architectural character has been lost because of first story modernization projects, inappropriate or even garish signs and the downtown urban renewal project that totally destroyed several blocks of these interesting storefronts.

Another important architectural element now missing from most of Dubuque's streets is the old cast iron street lights. They have been replaced by "modern" fixtures that are supposed to aid automobiles and deter crime. Few of the new lights, however, can match the old ones for their human scale, sense of architectural character and general urban design qualities. Hopefully, the few remaining cast iron street lights can be saved.

A Century of Dubuque Architecture

The Early Years, 1830-1860

Newman log cabin

The Early Years, 1830-1860

The Origins of Dubuque's Architectural Development

When the first permanent settlers arrived at Dubuque in 1833, local history records that they found a log cabin near what is now the intersection of Second and Locust in downtown Dubuque. The cabin was actually two buildings joined by a common roof covering a breezeway between them. It was constructed of square-hewed oak logs. Frequently called "dog-trot" cabins, such buildings were common in the South where climatic conditions help explain the concept. They often began as just one small structure, but as more room was needed, a second cabin was built facing the first, and the area between them covered to provide extra working space that was protected from the weather.

No one knows when this cabin was built, but it is known that William Newman occupied it during the 1830's, and that it was later owned by August A. Cooper. In Dubuque's early years the cabin served a variety of functions. Father Samuel Mazzuchelli once used it for a mass, and, on another occasion, the first governor of Iowa made a speech in it.

As time passed, the Newman cabin was covered with clapboards and more or less forgotten until 1915. In that year Frederick E. Bissell, Sr. rediscovered the cabin as it was being torn down. He was successful in raising $450.00 to purchase it and have it moved to Eagle Point Park where it stood until 1967 when the Dubuque County Historical Society moved it to its present location near the Mathias Ham Museum. Extensive restoration work was undertaken in conjunction with this last move.

It is somewhat of an American tradition to associate log cabins with the frontiers of pioneer settlement. Dubuque in 1833 was no exception. Perhaps as many as 100 log cabins were hastily erected by the miners during that first summer. Others built crude shanties, lived in tents or slept out-of-doors.

About the time Dubuque was being settled, steam-powered sawmills were becoming capable of producing boards in sufficient quantities to permit an important innovation in building construction. This was the "balloon frame", a system of building that consisted of wood framing nailed together and covered with sawed boards. To erect a balloon-framed house skilled craftsmen were not needed. Instead, a few men who knew how to use common tools could put one up in a short time. The whole system was made possible by the availability of machine-made nails in large quantities. When first developed, the nickname "balloon frame" was given to this building system because critics thought that such flimsy houses would fly away in the first strong wind.[1] To the contrary, they proved quite sturdy.

Prior to the introduction of the balloon frame method of construction, timber framing was usually used. Virtually unchanged since medieval times, timber framing relied on heavy beams mortised and pegged together then covered with hand-sawed clapboards. Construction was slow and required skilled carpenters.

In November, 1833, only five months after the first permanent settlers crossed the river to Dubuque, a raft of lumber from Wisconsin was brought downriver by William Lockwood. General Warner Lewis built the first frame house that same month, and Peter Lorimier built the second in December. These two buildings were later used by George W. Harrison as fixed points for his unofficial survey of the Dubuque mining region.

The summer of 1834 saw an increase in building activity at Dubuque. The town's first substantial structure, the Bell Tavern, was erected, partially of logs and partially of sawed lumber. Additional rafts of lumber were brought down from Wisconsin, and several other frame houses were built. Iowa's first church was also constructed in 1834 by local Methodists. It was located in present-day Washington Park. Peter Smith and William Clark were the builders. Their contract specified that the church was to be built of hewed logs, one story, twenty by twenty-six feet and ten feet high "in the clear." The completed church had a shingled roof and five windows. The cost—$225.00.[2]

While the Methodist Church was being built, a stone warehouse was also being constructed on the riverbank near the foot of Second Street. This was the

Iowa's first church, 1834

The first Saint Raphael's Church

first recorded use of native limestone as a construction material for a Dubuque building. Limestone carved from Dubuque's bluffs would continue to be a traditional construction material for many local buildings.

Growth was rapid for the next two years, and by 1836 Dubuque had about 1,000 residents, an undetermined number of houses, four taverns and more than sixty stores of various types. The first St. Raphael's church was also completed in 1836. It was the first local building that can be attributed to an identifiable architect, Father Samuel Mazzuchelli. Mazzuchelli was a Roman Catholic missionary who designed at least ten churches throughout the Upper Mississippi Valley. One of his most interesting churches is St. Augustine's, built in 1844 and still standing at New Diggings, Wisconsin.

A lack of lumber and shortage of skilled labor slowed the pace of construction, however, and Iowa's first newspaper, *The DuBuque Visitor*, noted in its premier issue of May 11, 1836 that:

> Artisans of almost every description are needed at DuBuque, and would find immediate employment and good wages, particularly brick-makers and masons.[3]

The first brick house was built by LeRoy Jackson in 1836, one of three erected along Main Street in that year. A mixture of eighteenth-century federal and colonial styles, Jackson's house was impressively large for the young community. It was probably designed and built by local craftsmen. There is no record of an architect being employed.

The Jackson house was undoubtedly an exception to most of the Dubuque residences constructed in 1836. Although a local sawmill had been established, its production could not meet the local demand and the quality of lumber was poor. It would take several more years before sufficient supplies of pine could regularly be brought down river from Wisconsin. Until good quality lumber became plentiful and local brickyards could be established, most Dubuque buildings were crude and ramshackle, the typical lot of a frontier mining location.

Despite continued growth and prosperity, a haphazard tradition of building continued until the late 1840's. Buildings were scattered at random, and little attention was given to architecture. In 1840 Solon Langworthy remarked that a traveler at the steamboat landing "could see no buildings better than hewn logs."[4] By that year the only brick commercial structure was the Jesse P. Farley and Company store. Boom town conditions do not usually contribute to a lasting architecture, and it is significant that the Newman log cabin, built before Dubuque was even established, has survived.

By mid-century, Dubuque was nearly twenty years old, and there was a rising interest in the city's appearance. The *Dubuque Miner's Express* noted in 1852:

> We take advantage of the opportunity which this notice affords us, to throw out some hints on the subject

of architectural style and variety in building. There is no subject perhaps, in which we could touch, that is more appropriate to new and rising towns than this. There is no feature in the exterior of a town or city, which clearly speaks the taste and character of its inhabitants as the architectural tone and style of their dwellings and public improvements. Show us neatness, elegance and taste in the style and symmetry of a dwelling, and we will form a very accurate idea of the taste and character of its inmates . . . In speaking of style, we cannot withhold the opinion that our western towns pay too little attention to variety . . . Nothing contributes so much to the beauty of any place as an emulous and chaste variety in the tone and style of its public improvements and private residences . . . Nothing will more readily win the admiration of the stranger or visitor, and nothing will more certainly decide the mind of him who is in search of a new home.[5]

The growth of the 1840's continued into the early 1850's. Vacant lots in the commercial district disappeared as larger, more substantial business buildings were constructed. Many earlier cabins and shanties were demolished to make way for new homes while others were moved, remodeled or rented. In 1854, 333 new buildings were constructed; in 1855 a total of 471 were built; and in 1856 over 500 new structures were erected, more than any previous year in Dubuque's history. Plans were made to build over 1,000 new structures in 1857, but the goal was not reached, due in part to a nationwide panic and depression.

By 1856 more than 125 residences had been built by Dubuque's wealthier citizens on the bluffs overlooking the town. A newspaper account recorded that:

> The bluffs in the rear of the city are becoming dotted all over with new residences, which seem, from points below, to be springing up out of the earth as the result of magic. It may be some trouble for the residents to get up to them, but then they are amply repaid for all their toil by the beautiful views and exhilarating breezes which continually are wafting o'er them.[6]

These bluff lots were in newly-platted additions, and their sale depended on the area being attractive.

During 1856 and 1857 the commercial district spread out to cover a four-block wide area between First and Seventh Streets. By 1856 the pace of construction had increased to the point where the city felt a need to regulate it. Dubuque's first construction ordinance "prescribed the manner in which large buildings should be constructed, with a view to prevent them from falling down."[7] At the same time another ordinance prohibited the construction of buildings with bay windows that projected more than two feet. The purpose of this ordinance was to control the projections, not so much for safety reasons, but because they obstructed street and sidewalk traffic.

Apparently, the concern over Dubuque's appearance expressed in 1852 by the *Dubuque Miner's Express*

Dubuque bluff development

was taken to heart by local citizens. Only four years later the newspaper recorded that:

> The buildings that are going up in the various parts of our city are of a superior character, much surpassing those constructed in previous years; and should the balance of the great number already under contract prove to be of the same description, they will greatly enhance the beauty of our city, and will challenge comparison with the architecture of any city of the West.[8]

The frontier mining camp years were clearly over, and Dubuque was becoming a prosperous city. Along with prosperity came abundant supplies of building materials, skilled craftsmen in all the building trades and the appearance of professional architects. For the first time in local history architecture was important. Examples of many different American architectural styles that developed during the first half of the nineteenth century appeared simultaneously in Dubuque between 1855 and 1860.

Early Buildings

Trained architects were rare on the midwestern frontier prior to mid-century. Instead, many buildings were erected by skilled craftsmen who relied upon their experience and the use of pattern books to construct almost any type of structure the client wanted. As a result, few buildings of this period can be attributed to specific designers. The lack of architects, however, did not prevent structures of every description from being built. Pattern books were readily available and widely circulated. They offered detailed descriptions and illustrations of the latest styles and fads of home construction. Builders often advertised their familiarity with the very latest architectural developments and proclaimed their proficiency in constructing any structure that was desired.

During the 1850's an incredible variety of buildings did appear in Dubuque but in the process many earlier structures were destroyed or altered beyond recognition. Fortunately, a few examples of early Dubuque's architecture have survived along with the major landmarks of the period. It is these "vernacular" buildings that provide the foundation for Dubuque's unique architectural heritage.

It was only by accident that the Newman log cabin was saved from demolition. Many other log houses were torn down to make way for the construction of commercial buildings. The flat terraces along the base of the bluffs were directly accessible to the river, the major travel route of the time. This prime land was needed for commerce and industry. To find remaining examples of early architecture one must look elsewhere, and Dubuque's lead mining origins offer clues about where to look. Most of the Dubuque mines were located amid the Mississippi River bluffs and coulees. Many miners wanted to live close to their workings, so they frequently built their cabins, shanties and houses near the base of the bluffs or along the coulees that led to the mines.

Stable behind 503 Southern Avenue

800 English Lane

Much later, city streets were routed up these same valleys. It is along these streets — Southern, Hill, University, Foye, Kaufmann, West Locust — to name a few, that some of the best examples of Dubuque's early vernacular architecture can be found.

It is unlikely that any more log cabins will be discovered hidden beneath a covering of clapboards. Several early stone buildings of great architectural interest, however, can still be found at various places around Dubuque. Without exception, these buildings represent masterful use of native construction materials and unusually skilled craftsmanship. The early stoneworking tradition in Dubuque probably stems from the influence of miners from Cornwall or other parts of Great Britain and Europe where building with stone had a long history. Throughout the lead mining region of Iowa, Wisconsin and Illinois, as well as in the copper and iron mining regions of northern Michigan, Minnesota and Wisconsin, similar native stone structures testify to the skill of these workers, many of whom migrated from the lead mines to the copper and iron mines as old workings were exhausted and new ones opened.

Perhaps Dubuque's most interesting stone buildings can be found along Southern Avenue. Behind 503 Southern is an old structure that originally was a stable for a nearby hotel. At present it merely serves as a storage shed. It is constructed entirely of rubble stone, randomly coursed and probably quarried nearby. Of particular interest are the heavy cut stone quoins that support the corners and the stone arches over the doors and windows. The building sits on a foundation of solid bedrock. While the stonework is not finely cut and fitted, this building is important because of the ingenious use of native building materials shown in its construction. The exact date of construction is not known, but it was probably built before 1850.

Nearby at 800 English Lane is one of Dubuque's finest stone houses. The two-story cottage is built into the hillside from which the stone was quarried. The construction is randomly-laid cut limestone precisely fitted with mortar. An interesting feature is the gallery porch across the front. John McMahon, a lead miner, reportedly built the house before 1840. It has been well cared for by its present owner, Mrs. Roseanne Wiedner. Just across the lane are remains of another stone structure that was never completed.

At 274 Southern Avenue is an excellent example of what has come to be known as "Riverboat Gothic" architecture. Built about 1855 by Henry Kelly, the house is a two-story stone and frame building with a full length gallery porch in front. Although still occupied as a residence, the building is threatened by industrial and commercial development on both sides. So-called "Riverboat Gothic" or "Steamboat Gothic" architecture characterized by ornate multi-level porches or galleries actually reflects a French influence carried northward along the Mississippi River from Louisiana and Saint Louis. Climatic conditions help explain the development of such covered porches. They prevented sunlight from beaming directly on the walls and provided a shaded place to rest on hot, humid evenings. Dubuque once had many "Riverboat Gothic" houses scattered along the bluffs. Several examples can still be found along Southern Avenue, West Third Street and Kirkwood Street. Some of these houses, such as the Jacob Michel house at 535 West Fifth Street, were in fact built after the Civil War. The Michel house was constructed in 1867. After passing through a succession of owners, its exterior has been restored and carefully maintained by the present owners, Dr. and Mrs. Earl Steininger. The characteristic galleried porches on many other "Riverboat Gothic" houses in Dubuque have been removed or enclosed during remodeling and modernization projects.

An unusual stone building can be found at 2105 Foye. Now empty, this building is said to have once housed a blacksmith shop, but little evidence remains to verify this use. The date of construction is not known. This two-story structure is built of rough-cut stone set in mortar. Of particular interest are the rounded arches above the two doors.

The original portion of the Mathias Ham Museum at Eagle Point is another significant stone house that will be discussed later.

Stone construction was not confined to domestic buildings in Dubuque. One of Dubuque's most famous landmarks is the old Shot Tower, built in 1856. The tower is 150 feet high. For the first 110 feet native limestone was used as a construction material while the top forty feet are brick. At its base the walls are three feet thick. It is one of only a few such towers left in the United States. Shot was made by melting lead in a small building at the foot of the tower. The molten lead was transported to the top by a windlass where it was poured through a series of screens at each of the nine levels. The lead dropped into cold water at the base to harden it. The rough shot was then polished by rotation in a cask, placed on an incline so it would roll through sieves to be sorted by size and finally packed in canvas bags for market. Although the Dubuque Shot Tower is no longer operable, it is still possible to see lead shot being made by a similar process at Tower Hill State Park in southwestern Wisconsin.

The history of the Dubuque Shot Tower is as interesting as the shot making process itself. At the time the tower was built, the Dubuque region supplied nearly all the lead for the Saint Louis shotmakers, Chadbourne and Forster, who had a monopoly in the Midwest shot market. Dubuque businessmen engaged the C. H. Rogers Co. to build and operate the tower in an attempt to break the Saint Louis monopoly. At first the Rogers Company was successful, but Chadbourne and Forster soon cut their prices below cost, an action Rogers could not match. In 1859 the tower was leased to Peli-Tallman Company for a few months before Cook and Langworthy undertook management. By this time, however, stockholders had become discouraged and

274 Southern Avenue (page 40)

willingly sold their shares for 5¢ and 10¢ on the dollar to local financier, J. K. Graves. At the outset of the Civil War, Graves announced in Saint Louis that he was making shot for the Union Army. His announcement alarmed the Chadbourne and Forster firm who sent a representative to Dubuque to buy the tower. In July, 1862 Graves sold out to the Saint Louis firm for $3,000 or about 50¢ on the dollar. The Dubuque *Daily Times* reported:

> The day before yesterday Messrs. Chadbourne and Forster paid $3000 for the Dubuque shot tower for the purpose of having a troublesome rival out of the way. Although they promised to expend $5000 on it and set it to work, in order to pacify many dissatisfied businessmen in the city, they of course do not intend to do any such thing. No, they privately informed their agents that they intend to board up the windows, take out the machinery, lock the door and throw the key into the river. Rather than have another sack of shot made in Dubuque, they said we will put a keg of powder under the tower and blow it higher than Gilderoy's kite.[9]

It was also reported that the day after the tower was purchased the wholesale price of shot increased 25¢ per sack. The Saint Louis Company made 1,000 sacks of shot per day. Thus, the price increase was sufficient to pay the purchase price of the Dubuque tower in only twelve working days.[10]

Although the bill of sale stipulated that Graves could not erect another shot tower in Dubuque, he led a group of local businessmen who continued to make shot for a number of years by using an abandoned mine shaft at the western edge of the city. Chadbourne and Forster were unsuccessful in stopping this operation.

In 1874 John Deery placed an equestrian statue of Andrew Jackson on top of the tower, but it was removed in 1881. Until 1911 the tower was used by the Standard Lumber Company as a watchtower. The disastrous riverfront fire of 1911 completely destroyed the inner framework and ladder of the tower. The abandoned structure was then allowed to deteriorate until 1959 when local citizens, with city assistance, raised $10,000 to stabilize and restore the old landmark. Although surrounded by riverfront industrial uses that make access difficult, Dubuque's old shot tower is one of the city's best-known historical sites and tourist attractions.

As early as 1836 brick was used as a construction material in Dubuque. Most of the earliest brick buildings have disappeared, but still standing at the corner of Fifth and Bluff is a two-story brick house that resembles the first brick house that LeRoy Jackson built in 1836. It was built during the late 1840's by J. H. Thedinga and was originally an addition to an earlier frame house that was demolished during the 1880's. Architecturally, the Thedinga house is a mixture of colonial and classical revival styles. It was allowed to deteriorate and was finally condemned in 1973. At that time the late Robert A. Sullivan acquired the property and rehabilitated the house for his residence. It was

Fifth and Bluff Streets

Shot Tower

Sullivan's fourth Dubuque renovation and was nearly completed at the time of his death in April, 1974. The Thedinga house is one of the city's oldest brick residences. Thedinga came from northern Germany in 1835 and settled in Dubuque in 1839. He was successful as a local businessman and also held several public offices. Thedinga was elected Dubuque's first German mayor in 1864; he also served as justice of the peace, was on the board of education and was chairman of the county board of supervisors.

Between the time the Thedinga house was built and the Shot Tower was completed, a number of architects arrived in Dubuque. By 1850 more people could afford the services of an architect and commissioned different ones to design houses and other buildings in many of the styles popular at the time. One early Dubuque architect, John Hill, advertised his services:

> Particular attention given to designs and building drawings with all their details and specifications on most reasonable terms.[11]

Hill declared his firm to be skilled in all the architectural styles of the day.

By 1857 there were twelve architects listed in the city directory. Six of these men were also cross-referenced as builders. While questions could be raised about the professional training of many early Dubuque architects, a number of outstanding local landmarks were designed by them.

At mid-century the architectural development of Dubuque had reached a crossroad. The era of anonymous mining frontier architecture had ended. Between 1850 and 1860 local architects gave Dubuque structures that were designed in many of the revival styles popular at the time. In 1856 and 1857 alone, public buildings and residences in the Greek Revival, Gothic Revival, Egyptian Revival, Italian Villa and Octagon styles were under construction in Dubuque. Significantly, some of the major examples have survived.

Architectural Developments at Mid-Century

Greek Revival architecture appeared in the United States around 1800 and large numbers of Greek temple courthouses, markets, houses and other buildings were constructed during the first half of the nineteenth century. In most areas the peak period of Greek Revival construction was the 1830's and 1840's. The style became so popular that some critics complained of its repetition.

> One such temple well placed in a wood might be a pleasant object enough; but to see a river lined with them, with children trundling hoops before their doors, beef carried into their kitchens and smoke issuing moreover from those unclassical objects, is too much even for high taste.[12]

Generally, Greek Revival structures are of rectangular shape but some examples are square in plan. The fluted columns topped by capitals in the various classical Greek "orders" is a key characteristic of the style. Wall surfaces on Greek Revival buildings are usually as smooth as the construction material allows. Roofs are low or flat, and dormer windows are rare. Architects took many liberties, however, with the classical orders, often omitting the fluting from columns, substituting square pillars for round columns or making other modifications for one kind of practical reason or another.

The development of Greek Revival architecture on the agricultural plains of the Midwest did not reach the same levels of purity found in New England, the South or the old Northwest, but in places like Dubuque, Greek Revival buildings varied from elaborate pillared mansions to simple brick cottages with only a hint of Greek detail along the eave or gable. In some instances the scale and setting of Greek Revival buildings made them imposing landmarks.

One of Dubuque's most impressive houses with Greek Revival features was built in 1856 by Joseph A. Rhomberg at 508 West Seventh Street. Besides his interests in real estate and railroads, Rhomberg was a wine merchant, and the entire bluff in front of his house was once covered with terraced vineyards, the remains of which can still be seen. Rhomberg's house is now a mixture of Greek Revival and Italian Villa architecture but once possessed "Riverboat Gothic" detail as well. It is square in plan and once had a belvedere on the roof. The columned facade has also been altered. Originally, both the first and second stories had decks with ornamental railings, and there were six instead of four columns. One of the building's most interesting features is a wine cellar that extends beneath West Seventh Street.

In 1856 Solon Langworthy built an imposing Greek Revival house overlooking the city and river at what is now 264 Alpine Street. What is actually the rear of the house faces the street. A columned portico overlooks a sloping lawn toward the river. Today the house is

J. A. Rhomberg house on the bluff

J. A. Rhomberg house, 508 West Seventh Street

T-shaped in plan, but it is likely that the wing extending to Alpine Street is a later addition to the original rectangular building. At the time it was built, the Solon Langworthy house was surrounded by acres of grounds, but the land was subdivided after Langworthy's death. The house is now used for apartments.

Nationally, the Greek Revival style had lost much of its popularity by the time it reached Dubuque. Although several important examples, including the Rhomberg and Langworthy houses, were built during the 1850's, many other local buildings possessing Greek Revival characteristics were, in fact, not built until after the Civil War.

Gable treatments, entries and other Greek Revival details are common on many buildings throughout Dubuque. The classical portico is also found. Among some of the more interesting examples are the old Welbes family house at 2615 Hillcrest and residences at 855 South Grandview, 1323-25 Bluff, 3035 Pennsylvania, 2452 Broadway, 713 Lincoln, 1204 Mount Loretta and 1163 Highland.

The rising interest in Gothic Revival architecture was one reason why the Greek Revival style became less popular by mid-century. Gothic Revival structures had been built in the United States as early as 1820, but it was not until the 1840's and 1850's that the style's popularity was assured. During the 1840's Alexander

Solon Langworthy house, 264 Alpine Street (page 46)

2105 Foye Street (page 42)

2452 Broadway Street

713 Lincoln Avenue

1204 Mount Loretta Avenue

3035 Pennsylvania Avenue

2615 Hillcrest Road

Jackson Davis became the country's most prolific Gothic Revival architect. He originated the concept of the country cottage characterized by steep roofs, spacious verandas, a dominant central gable and "gingerbread" ornament. At the same time James Renwick, Jr. and Richard Upjohn produced designs for Gothic churches that made them the leading ecclesiastical architects of their time and set the pattern for much American church building into the twentieth century.

Architecturally, the almost universal element of the Gothic Revival style is the pointed arch. Steep pointed gables, verandas, towers or turrets, window tracery and "gingerbread" trim along eaves and gables are other common features. Unlike Greek Revival architecture, there are no "rules" to be followed, and Gothic Revival houses show a wide variety of shapes, sizes and the amount of ornament.

In addition to "country houses" the Gothic Revival style of architecture was particularly suitable for churches. Dubuque's best example of the style is the Cathedral of Saint Raphael, designed and built between 1852 and 1859 by a local architect of Irish ancestry, John Mullany. Perhaps the most important public building of the 1850's, Saint Raphael's is 85 by 125 feet and can accommodate 1,200 persons. Of special architectural interest is the finely detailed window tracery and the monochromatic appearance of the facade, both key elements of Gothic Revival church architecture. Although the church itself was completed in 1859, it took sixty years to finish additions and installations of furnishings. The tower was added in 1876. It was planned to be 300 feet tall but structural settling prevented its completion. It is modeled after Magdalen College, Oxford. In 1886

Edward Langworthy octagon house, Third and Alpine Streets (page 60)

Cathedral of Saint Raphael

an Italian artist Luigi Gregori, was commissioned to paint the interior during a remodeling project. His paintings show the Holy Ghost, Isaiah, John the Baptist and several saints. The present stained glass windows were installed in 1886. They were imported from London and represent two epochs of world history — the Old and New Testaments. The four bells, donated by members of the congregation, were dedicated in 1897. They cost $2,000. In 1919 the original organ was replaced with a new instrument that was the largest of its kind in Iowa. Along with the adjoining rectory, Saint Raphael's has been carefully maintained as the archdiocesan cathedral for over a century.

In addition to being one of Iowa's best examples of Gothic Revival church architecture, the building of Saint Raphael's also represents an early exercise in town planning and urban design. At the time of its construction, Dubuque's main steamboat dock was at the base of Second Street, and the downtown was centered at Second and Main. Second Street was purposely built ninety feet wide to provide a dramatic vista of the Cathedral as one walked from the docks to downtown. The church's location at the head of Second Street made it the major focal point of downtown Dubuque.

The construction of Saint Raphael's apparently assured Mullany's position as a prominent local architect for at least a few years. In 1860 he advertised in the City Directory:

John Mullany
Architect and Builder
is prepared at all times to plan and design both
Public and Private Buildings
in any of the
Orders and Styles of Architecture
and will
Contract or Superintend the Erection of the Same
Satisfaction Warranted.[13]

A few years later he was chosen by the German Catholic congregation to design the new Saint Mary's Church.

One of the most unusual structures of Gothic origin in Dubuque is Lady of Lourdes Nursing Home located at the head of Iowa Street. The original concept for this building was based on a Gothic Revival plan, but as it was built and altered, elements of other styles were added. No architect is known.

Today it is impossible to describe Lady of Lourdes in terms of a single architectural style. The conjectural sketch shows pointed Gothic windows and two one-story wings. As built, the windows in the towers were rounded in the Romanesque manner, and the wings were two stories. Later the "onion dome" caps on the towers and much of the ornament were removed.

The history of this building is as unusual as its architecture. It was constructed in 1854 to house the Dubuque Female College, an institution sponsored by

Catherine Beecher of the famous New England family. She offered Dubuque $20,000 in cash, $1,000 worth of books and equipment and four faculty members if the town would erect the building and recruit students. The college lasted until 1859 when the building became the Dubuque public high school. In 1862 it became a private school of "higher class" and in 1864 was taken over by the Episcopalians as the Lee Female Seminary. Eight years later the Presbyterians bought it and opened the Presbyterian Theological School which was the forerunner of the University of Dubuque. In 1907 the Catholics purchased the building and remodeled it for use as the first Immaculate Conception School. In 1925 this school was moved to its Davis Street location and the building became a home for women. It also housed a music school under the direction of the Sisters of Saint Francis. For the last several decades the old Dubuque Female College building was known as Lady of Lourdes Nursing Home. It is now a recreation center for girls.

Gothic Revival houses were not common in Dubuque. The most elaborate example was built in 1857 by Frederick E. Bissell but does not survive.[14] None of the few examples date from the pre-Civil War period. The city's best remaining Gothic cottage is at 1207 Grove Terrace and was built in 1890 by Dubuque businessman Benton M. Harger. His company, Harger and Blish, was a leading book, stationery and wallpaper store around the turn of the century. Later the house was owned by Mary Lee, a daughter of Patrick J. Lee

Lady of Lourdes (1975)

Lady of Lourdes (1880's)

1207 Grove Terrace

who was president of the Citizen's State Bank. The present owner is noted Iowa artist, Frank Licciardi. Nestled in its wooded bluffside setting, the Harger house has all the character that Davis' and Downing's country cottages were meant to possess. Along with its steeply-pointed gables, the lacelike bargeboards, saw-cut brackets under the eaves, spacious porches and ornamental brickwork are the building's distinguishing architectural features.

Two other Gothic Revival houses can be found at 863 West Fifth Street and 1206 Prairie Street. The Prairie Street house has been re-sided, and on both the detail is less ornate than on the Harger house. The overall appearance of these smaller houses is more subdued. Although vertical board and batten siding was commonly used on Gothic Revival houses, none of the Dubuque examples employ this method of construction.

Several of Dubuque's most architecturally diverse and significant landmark buildings were built in 1857 and 1858. The Dubuque City Hall, Dubuque County Jail, Bissell-Babbage-Andrew-McDonald house and Edward Langworthy Octagon house were all designed by John Francis Rague, who was probably the single most important architect to work in Dubuque during the nineteenth century.

Ragne was born in New Jersey in 1799 and received his architectural training at the New York offices of Minard Lafever. After working in New York

863 West Fifth Street

1206 Prairie Street

for a few years, he moved to Springfield, Illinois where he soon became President of the Mechanic's Institute, a leader of a church choir, city market master and owner of a bakery. Among others in the choir were Mary Todd, Abraham Lincoln, Stephan A. Douglas and a young lady who later became Rague's first wife. In 1836 he was elected a town trustee. During the following year the decision was made to construct a new state house and Rague was chosen as the supervising architect.[15] In 1839 he was asked to draw plans for the first capitol of Iowa at Iowa City. The Greek Revival structure has been restored and still stands as part of the University of Iowa. Domestic and business difficulties forced Rague to move to Milwaukee in 1844. During the next several years he designed buildings at Milwaukee, Chicago, Madison and Janesville. Among his contracts were three buildings for the University of Wisconsin: Bascom Hall, North Hall and South Hall. By 1854 Rague had remarried and moved to Dubuque where he lived until his death in 1877.

Rague's most unusual Dubuque building is the County Jail. Built in 1857-1858, it was the last known example of Egyptian Revival architecture erected in the United States. Architecturally, it is probably the single most significant building in Dubuque because of its rarity. Less than fifty Egyptian Revival structures were ever built.[16]

The Egyptian Revival style flourished briefly between 1830 and 1850. Because of its exoticism, it was never very popular. Most of the buildings designed in the style were prisons, the most famous of which was the New York Halls of Justice better known as "The Tombs". No Egyptian Revival houses are known to have been built, but the style was used for a court house in Newark, New Jersey, a medical school in Virginia, a cemetery entrance in Connecticut, churches in New York and Tennessee, an insurance office in Philadelphia and a railroad station in Massachusetts.

Few styles of nineteenth century architecture are easier to identify. Every Egyptian Revival building has at least one of the following characteristics: walls with an inclined face, a curved or roll cornice, window frames that narrow upward, columns that bulge or represent bundles of stalks tied together with horizontal bands, and the vulture and sun disk symbol.

The Dubuque County Jail is an outstanding example of the style. It is built of rough surfaced gray limestone with cast-iron window and door frames. The traditional Egyptian columns flank the entrance and a few sun disc symbols can still be seen above windows. The others have disappeared. The jail is three stories with an overall size of 36' x 54'. There were three tiers of cells each 4' 4" x 10' with a catwalk providing entry to the upper cells. Use of the building for jail purposes ended in 1971 and its future is uncertain although there is interest in adapting it for use as a cultural center. The building was listed on the National Register of Historic Places in 1972.

The Dubuque City Hall is radically different from Rague's County Jail design. Often compared to Boston's Faneuil Hall, the building's prototype was actually the old Fulton Market in New York City. It was built in 1857-1858 "with great care and expense to provide a market house of immense convenience and ornament to our city."[17] When construction began, the estimated cost was $32,500 but at completion the final cost had risen to $50,000. The concept of the building provided a rare combination of city office space and market house following a tradition dating back to medieval times. Originally, the basement housed a police station and jail while the first floor was used for markets. Each window marked a stall and they extended all the way to the floor to allow wagons to back up and unload goods. On the second floor were city offices, and the third floor was used as a public hall and ballroom. The overall building dimensions are 152' x 50', and it is 68' high.

The construction is of brick and wood. Architecturally, the Dubuque City Hall is based on eighteenth century colonial concepts mixed with mid-nineteenth century elements. The bracketed eaves and ornate cupola that was removed in 1954 suggest Italianate influence. The bell in front of the building once hung in the cupola and tolled for church services, fires and curfews. Although the market function of City Hall ended many years ago, it is still used for Dubuque's city administration offices. It too is listed on the National Register of Historic Places.

Dubuque City Hall

Of all the houses in Dubuque, none has received more attention than the Edward Langworthy Octagon house, designed by Rague and constructed in 1857. Virtually all of the octagon houses in the United States were erected between 1848 and 1860 and were inspired by Orson S. Fowler's book, *A Home for All, or the Gravel Wall and Octagon Mode of Building.*

Fowler was a phrenologist, amateur architect and marriage analyst.

> Fowler was a man in the grand and continuing American tradition of spellbinding crackpots. His specialty was phrenology, the pseudo-science of reading character from skull bumps. Fowler also wrote *Sexual Science* a frank marriage manual of 930 pages. Putting into practice his theories, Fowler was married three times and he fathered three children when he was over seventy years old. Fowler did not actually invent the octagon house; there had been polygonal buildings for centuries, including some eight-sided churches, meeting houses, schools, tollhouses and barns in the U.S. He pointed out the undeniable fact that eight walls enclose more space than four walls of the same length, and insisted that an octagonal house was the one answer to each and every building problem.[18]

In his book on octagon building, Fowler cites the fact that an octagon structure encloses twenty percent more space than a square with the same total length of wall. He also noted the octagon design's compactness and greater efficiency for heating and ventilating. Fowler was one of the first Americans to encourage the use of concrete (the gravel wall) as a basic construction material and to plan for central heating, gas lighting, hot and cold running water and indoor flush toilets. In addition, Fowler was not unaware of the octagon's aesthetic qualities:

> Scarcely less important is its greater beauty, which is due to its approaching more closely the sphere, the predominant or governing form of nature.[19]

A large number of octagon houses were built using nearly every material. In Iowa alone there are over twenty still standing. The Langworthy house is actually the second octagon home that was built in Dubuque; the first was torn down in 1932.[20]

Edward Langworthy built his octagon house of red brick from his own brickyard. Each wall is double and the frames are of hand-hewed timber. The central hall and formal parlor is 20' x 40' and runs the full length of the north half of the first floor. Reception and sitting rooms are on the south half of the first floor. The second floor has corner bedrooms and family rooms. The total cost of construction was $8,000. Many of the original furnishings came from Europe via New Orleans and the Mississippi River. They included a rosewood piano, carved rosewood sofas and chairs upholstered with rose satin brocade, floor length mirrors in gilt frames, six white marble fireplaces, chandeliers of French bronze

Dubuque County Jail (page 58)

with gold leaf and a parlor carpet from Brussels specially sewed to fit the room. The present owner, a great-grandson of Edward Langworthy has carefully maintained the house since 1946. The formal parlor has been preserved in its original state, and most of the furnishings are intact. The Edward Langworthy house was recorded by the Historic American Buildings Survey in 1934 and has been nominated to the National Register of Historic Places.

Other Dubuque buildings designed by Rague included the Bissell-Babbage-Andrew-McDonald house, an imposing Gothic Revival edifice that has been destroyed, and the First Ward (Franklin), Third Ward (Prescott) and Fifth Ward (Audubon) Schools. The Goodrich-Wilson-Ryan house at 1243 Locust is also attributed to Rague.

Even while Rague was designing Egyptian jails and octagon houses in Dubuque, other local architects were erecting buildings in other revival styles. Among the most significant were several Italian Villa houses that provided an architectural basis for many other post-Civil War Victorian homes in the same style.

Italian Villa (or Italianate, Tuscan Villa, and Bracketed as the style is also known) architecture received its inspiration from the anonymous farmhouse architecture of the Italian countryside. The first American design in the style appeared at Burlington, New Jersey in 1837. By 1850 the style had become the major non-Gothic style of the picturesque movement and was popularized by Andrew Jackson Downing and Alexander Jackson Davis in their books. Key elements include bay windows, balconies and verandas, wide bracketed eaves and square towers. Towers stand at an off-center location, and if none is present, there is usually a belvedere. Wall surfaces are smooth and uniform with any rustication confined to quoins. Roofs are of slight pitch, gabled, or hipped. Windows are often grouped in twos or threes and are commonly round headed. Brick, stone and wood are all used as construction materials and the amount of ornament varies greatly from house to house.

The Italian Villa style was rarely used for nonresidential structures, but much of its popularity stems from the fact that buildings constructed in the style were simultaneously picturesque and practical.

Writing of the Italian Villa style John Maass noted that:

> None of the cliches about dark, gloomy, fussy Victorian mansions can possibly be applied to these high, wide and handsome homes. There is a timeless air of good design and good taste about these amazingly modern houses . . . The most delightful parts are the towers; they are frankly for pleasure, affording a cool retreat where the breeze blows unmolested and whence a cheerful and extended prospect is commanded.[21]

One of Dubuque's most interesting Italian Villa houses was built at Eagle Point in 1857 by Mathias Ham. Ham was a native of Kentucky who arrived at

Dubuque with the first wave of lead miners in 1833. During the next few years he acquired 25,000 acres of land along the Mississippi and developed interests in a variety of business enterprises that included brickmaking, lime kilns, contracting, shipping and cabbage growing. Because much of his cabbage was used for making sauerkraut, Ham acquired the nickname "Sauerkraut King."

The house Ham constructed at Eagle Point in 1857 was actually an addition to a five room cottage he had built in 1839 of native stone from the nearby bluffs. The "addition" consisted of sixteen rooms. The first floor has a central hall and four large rooms with fourteen foot ceilings that feature molded plaster rosettes and mouldings. There are five rooms on the second floor and seven on the third. An octagonal belvedere, reached by a spiral stairway from the third floor, provides a fine view of the river. Woodwork used in the house includes pine flooring and carved walnut stair rails, newel posts and spindles. The exterior is of limestone from Nauvoo, Illinois. Ham had the subcontract to supply stone for the Dubuque Custom House, and much of the stone used in his house was rejected pieces from that project. It has been reported that some of the stone Ham brought from Nauvoo was taken from the ruins of the Mormon Temple there. No record exists of the architect Ham employed to design his house.

There are many stories and legends connected with the Ham family, none of which have been proven true. One legend tells of the house being haunted because of a murder being committed there. Other stories recount river pirates and whiskey smugglers using the belvedere as a lookout. All of these tales have been well told in a book by John A. Baule entitled, *The Ham House and the Life of Its Builder.*[22]

Mathias Ham lived in the house until his death in 1889, and two of his daughters continued to reside there for many years afterwards. Between Ham's death and the time the Dubuque County Historical Society took over the building in 1964, it had served a number of functions including the Dr. Kegler Cancer Cure Hospital and the Dubuque Park Board offices. Since occupying the building the Dubuque County Historical Society has completed extensive restoration work to the first floor rooms. It is once again possible to feel the spacious elegance of this Dubuque landmark in somewhat the manner it was during the years when it was the scene of many gay parties. The exterior of the house is virtually unchanged, with the exception of a missing railing above the front entrance and the third floor dormer windows that were added sometime after 1900.

Another important Italian Villa house was built by General Warner Lewis in 1854 at 325 Alpine Street. The architect is unknown but interestingly enough, Lewis' house was originally built in the colonial Federal style, and the Italian Villa cupola, bracketed eaves and bay windows were not added until after 1900 by John

Mathias Ham house, Shiras Street and Lincoln Avenue

T. Adams. One of Dubuque's finest carriage houses stands on the spacious wooded lot.

General Lewis was another one of Dubuque's first settlers, arriving in 1833 after serving as aide to General Henry Dodge during the Blackhawk War. He was appointed surveyor general of Iowa, Wisconsin and Minnesota by presidents Polk, Pierce and Buchanan. Lewis also held several local offices and was elected Dubuque County representative to the Wisconsin Territorial Legislature. He later served in the Iowa legislature.

Between 1861 and Adams' purchase of it in 1904, the house passed through the hands of several owners. Adams was president of Carr, Ryder and Adams Co. and also played a major role in national politics. He managed President Taft's campaign in Iowa, was national chairman of the Republican party during Warren Harding's election and was party chairman until after Calvin Coolidge's election in 1924. During this period he became known as the "maker of presidents." For many years the historic Lewis-Adams house has been owned by Mr. and Mrs. Frederick E. Bissell, Jr.

The Frederick Weigel house at 1192 Locust Street is another example of Italian Villa architecture that was arrived at in successive stages. The rear of the house was built in 1854-1855. The front section, now the main portion of the house, was completed shortly after 1860 by pioneer Dubuque contractor Rufus Rittenhouse. The architect of the original portion is not known but

Lewis-Adams house, 325 Alpine Street

may have been Robert Rogers, a master builder who taught Rittenhouse. Five generations of Weigels have lived in the house, and it is still occupied by a descendant. Frederick Weigel was born in Wittenburg, Germany, in 1819. He arrived at Dubuque in June, 1833 with his parents and three sisters. Weigel became prominent in milling, meat packing and real estate, purchasing a large amount of downtown real estate, much of which is still owned by descendants. Weigel's house was furnished with hand-carved furniture, some pieces inlaid with gold, antique silver and china and valuable works of art.

Another significant Italian Villa built between 1855 and 1860 is at 597 Loras Boulevard. This square wood-frame house possesses many traditional Italianate architectural characteristics including rounded windows, a hipped roof, wide bracketed eaves and a square belvedere. The house has twelve rooms and forty-two windows, many of which reach from floor to ceiling. Its recent owners have undertaken extensive restoration work.

1192 Locust Street

The development of Italian Villa architecture and construction generally in Dubuque, was slowed by the Panic of 1857 and the Civil War. Although many landmark structures were erected before 1860, Dubuque's architectural development reached its peak during the decades between the Civil War and the turn of the century.

Early landmarks and exotic curiosities aside, much of Dubuque's present character was formed during the high Victorian era of the seventies, eighties and nineties. Compared to the florid designs that were to come, the Italian Villas of the 1850's were plain, early expressions of faith by a community emerging from its frontier mining camp origins into an era of growth and prosperity. Simple shelter was no longer the major concern. By 1860 Dubuque was maturing into a confident city.

597 Loras Boulevard

A Century of Dubuque Architecture

The Victorian Years, 1860-1890

The Victorian Years, 1860-1890

Post Civil War Dubuque and the Victorian Age

The flurry of building that was under way in 1857 slowed as the nationwide financial panic and depression of that year struck Dubuque. Some of the buildings under construction were finished but others, such as the Dubuque Custom House and Post Office, were delayed by the depression only to have the outbreak of the Civil War further postpone completion. In the case of the Custom House, for example, the end of construction was delayed until 1866 causing the final cost to be more than double the original 1857 estimate. The year 1857 was predicted to be the biggest construction year in Dubuque's history and the prospects for the following year were to be even better. In fact, fewer buildings were completed in 1857 than in 1856. Some local residents had to sell the new houses they had contracted to build just before the panic struck.

Recovery from the Panic of 1857 was well under way before the outbreak of the Civil War in 1860. Somewhat surprisingly, there were more architects listed in the 1860 Dubuque city directory than in 1857. Many were new listings, with only half of the architects listed in 1857 appearing in 1860. Apparently there was confidence that the decade of the 1860's would be a time of great growth and prosperity. The Civil War, however, proved to have a far deeper impact than was probably expected. Between 1860 and 1865 the number of architects in Dubuque dropped from fourteen to three.

Generally, it took until the late 1860's for local economic conditions and construction activity to return to "normal". When this happened, Dubuque embarked upon a period of varied architectural development that probably rivaled anything seen in any other Midwestern community of comparable size. The 1870's were the peak of what is traditionally called the Victorian Age.

Historically, the Victorian age is dated from the coronation of England's Queen Victoria in 1837 to her death in 1901. Architecturally, the Victorian period is usually regarded as the forty years between 1840 and 1880. This period approximates the first industrial age in America, an era that saw the development of the telegraph, ocean steamer, modern machine tools, farm machinery, petroleum fuels, sewing machine, rotary printing press, gas lights, electric motor, telephone and electric lighting. The growth of the American railway system was one of the most visible and dramatic accomplishments of the period. In 1840 there were less than 3,000 miles of railroads in the United States; in 1880 there were 95,000 miles.

In the strictest sense most of the buildings erected in Dubuque prior to about 1900 could be correctly labeled "Victorian." Such a general term, however, would not be very descriptive of the varied architectural styles that appeared in Dubuque between 1860 and 1890, or for that matter between 1840 and 1900.

In contrast to many of today's buildings "that stand on the shifting quicksand of insecurity, Victorian architecture was founded on the rock of superb confidence."[1] Such confidence was accompanied by a sense of pride and interest in beauty that has become uncommon.

Both large and small communities took great pride in a new public building; it would be described as "artistic", "a noble speciman of architecture" or "an ornament to our fair city". This Victorian civic spirit represents an interesting contrast to our present brand of boasting which is only concerned with size and cost.[2]

Dubuque was no exception for the 1886 *Dubuque Business Annual* discusses the city's architectural progress at some length:

> One of the most gratifying features of Dubuque, taken in connection with its present rapid growth, is the fine appearance of its architecture. In earlier and pioneer days but little attention was bestowed in this direction, and some landmarks still remain of the time when everyone was necessarily to a great extent his own architect. But these are fast disappearing; and some of them, though really valuable and useful structures, have been torn down to make way for better ones which were found profitable as well as desirable under the circumstances of increased value of ground and favorable prices at which better material, more choice construction, and superior designs are now attainable. Ordinarily, the man who, being non-professional, or at most only an amateur, does his own planning, pays dearly for the supposed economy, as a skilled architect more than earns his fees in the gain of room and saving of material as well as the better arrangement of conveniences, to say nothing of the improved symmetry of form and beauty of appearance imparted by his skill. The mistake is serious; and yet its commission is found everywhere, though there is a general diffusion in the land of much information and taste concerning architecture. In the Dubuque of today it is pleasant to say, that architecture is not neglected. During the last decade great attention has been paid to this handmaid of modern civilization. Residing here are first class representatives of this important and useful art. Throughout the city, in the outskirts and in more central locations, are to be seen phases of architecture having a commendable expression in cozy cottage, villa-mansion, elegant store, stately public building and grand church edifice. Mostly prevalent are the irregular Italian Style and modifications of the Gothic. These are perhaps the most useful types to analyze and adapt to this latitude and climate.[3]

The "Italian and Gothic" styles were found in post Civil War Dubuque, to be sure, but the catalog of architectural styles for the period between 1860 and 1890 would have to include the Second Empire, Queen Anne, High Victorian Gothic, High Victorian Italianate and Stick Styles as well.

In any year between 1860 and 1890 there were as few as three or as many as fourteen architects listed in the city directories. The most prominent local architects during the seventies and eighties were Fridolin J. Heer, Charles A. Wilbur, F. D. Hyde and Thomas T. Carkeek. These men were responsible for a large number of Dubuque buildings including most of the major landmarks from this period. Fridolin Heer and his son emerged as perhaps the leading local architects from about 1880 to as late as 1934.

Architectural schooling in the modern sense was not common until the 1880's. Many architects received their training as draftsmen or "apprentices" in the offices of other architects who probably had learned in the same manner. Throughout the thirty year period after 1860, many Dubuque architects also continued the practice of being contractors, surveyors, cabinetmakers, art teachers or illustrators. Fridolin Heer worked as a master stonecutter and mason before turning to architecture in 1870. C. A. Wilbur was both an architect and builder, and as late as 1885 John Keenan advertised in the city directory.

John Keenan
Architect
Contractor and Superintendent
also agent for
Reedy's Improved Patent Steam
Hydraulic and Hand Power Elevators[4]

Even John F. Rague, the pre-eminent local architect of the 1850's, was a part-time agent for the Iowa Iron Works, makers of cast iron building facades.

Continuing Trends in Local Architecture

During the early 1860's William Ryan moved to Dubuque from his boyhood home at Galena. Ryan was a meatpacker and close friend of Ulysses S. Grant. With the help of Grant, Ryan received large contracts to supply meat to the Union Army during the Civil War. As a result, Ryan became wealthy and established the basis for Dubuque's meat packing industry.

About ten years after moving to Dubuque, Ryan built an Italian Villa house at 1389 Locust for his first family. In 1888 he bought the house next door at 1375 Locust from John Thompson, a Dubuque mayor who had built it in 1870. Ryan moved his second wife and children into the house he bought from Thompson. The two "Ryan" houses are among the finest Italian Villas ever constructed in Dubuque. Although the house at 1389 Locust is less elaborate than the Thompson-Ryan house next door, it possesses many traditional Italian Villa characteristics including the finely-proportioned square tower, rounded hoods over the windows, bracketed eaves, corbeled chimneys and a low-pitched roof that is partly gabled and partly hipped. Now used for apartments, the house is well maintained and architecturally intact with the exception of a missing second floor balcony that once could be reached from a door in the tower.

In contrast to Ryan's first house, the Thompson-Ryan house at 1375 Locust has architectural detail found on no other Italian Villa house in Dubuque. The

541 West Third Street

elaborate window trim and finely proportioned mansard roof are exceptional, and the tall belvedere topped with cast iron cresting is a Dubuque landmark. The lavish interior has also been maintained in all its Victorian elegance. The house was owned by members of the Ryan family until the 1960's. In 1967 it was purchased and restored by Robert A. Sullivan. For the past several years it has been owned by a group of Dubuque residents who have opened it to the public as a restaurant. In addition it is still possible to see such unusual details as the carved marble likeness of Mayor Thompson's daughter on one of the fireplaces, the ornamental hardware on the doors and the gateposts with General Grant's profile cast in iron. Ryan reportedly had these specially made as a tribute to his old friend who was a frequent visitor at the house.

William Ryan died in 1890, but his wife lived in the house at 1375 Locust until the early 1920's. Their daughters, Misses Alice and Helen Ryan, occupied the house until the late 1960's. There are many stories associated with the Ryan family including persistent tales about Miss Helen taking a taxi to Chicago for a shopping trip during the Great Depression of the 1930's or going to Cedar Rapids by cab to have her hair done.

There are several other Dubuque houses of Italian Villa design that are worth mentioning. Among the more interesting are the Joseph J. Steil house at 541 West Third Street, and residences at 1330 Locust, 1871 North Main and 333 Villa Street. The Steil house was built during the 1870's as a Ladies' Episcopal Seminary but was long inhabited by the Joseph Steil family. One of his children reportedly used the tower as a place of escape to practice his violin. Like the house on North Main, Steil's house is an excellent example of Italian Villa architecture with its L-shaped plan, gabled roof and well-proportioned tower rising from the corner of the L. Both houses are sited to provide fine views of downtown and the river. Situated high on the very edge of a Dubuque bluff the house on Villa Street also provides a view for many miles both up and down the river. The present owners, Dr. and Mrs. James Pearson, are in the process of completing extensive restoration work.

Italian Villa houses continued to be built in Dubuque until late in the nineteenth century. Paralleling the national trend, the earlier local examples were typically dignified homes of wealthy men. Later, characteristics of the style were translated into less costly and less elaborate houses often portraying many variations on the same design theme.

In a 1911 publication the Dubuque Chamber of Commerce wrote:

> One of the features that characterize Dubuque is the attractive and substantial houses in which the workmen dwell. A remarkably large percentage own their own homes which bespeaks a prosperous condition. There are many desirable sites not far removed from the manufacturing districts that afford sufficient lawn space, fresh air and easy access to public schools. Many of these homes boast of a thrifty little garden spot.[5]

The Ryan houses

333 Villa Street

1330 Locust Street

1871 North Main Street

Usually "designed" by local masons or contractors instead of architects, these structures represent a significant architectural collection that contributes much to the overall character of the city.

Dubuque's "vernacular" structures possess general characteristics and specific details from a variety of different styles, but in summarizing their architectural development, there are a number of common features. Brick is almost universally used as the major construction material. This traditional use of brick probably reflects elements of Dubuque's ethnic background as well as the relative availability of materials and construction costs at the time. Typically, these houses are rectangular in plan. The overall appearance is symmetrical or even classical in proportion. Whatever detail is present is usually taken from Greek Revival architecture and consists of gable treatments or a row of dentils along an eave. One and one-half or two story heights are most common. Entrances are found on either the gable ends or the sides. Additions are usually placed at the rear or as an L-shaped wing off one side. Gabled roofs are most common, but other roof shapes were also frequently used. Dormers can be seen on many houses. Chimneys vary greatly in height and shape and are usually plain. A few elaborately corbeled examples, however, can be found. Porches are very common. Everything from simple covered stoops to pillared, full-width galleries are seen. A unique feature found on many Dubuque houses of this type is a two-story porch set into a rear corner of the house. These porches are often screened.

One of the most interesting aspects of Dubuque's vernacular buildings is their windows. The windows themselves are usually double-hung types of rectangular shape. In earlier houses simple brick arch lintels appear, but in many of the structures built during the seventies and eighties elaborate stone lintels were used. Produced by local stonecutters they often have carved ornament of baroque-like richness. In looking into the background of several stonecutters who worked in Dubuque during the 1870's and 1880's, one finds that Fridolin Heer and Andrew Pfiffner came from Switzerland, August Jungk came from Saxony, Bernhard Schulte came from Westphalia, John Meyers learned the trade in Prussia and Peter Mihm was from Bavaria. Whether the individual draftsmen produced designs reminiscent of their native environments is not known, but the great variety of exceptionally carved stone lintels is one of the unique elements of Dubuque's architectural heritage.

There are literally hundreds of these "vernacular" houses in Dubuque. They are found in all parts of the city. Many earlier examples can be seen in the Washington Street neighborhood and in the vicinity of the Cathedral of Saint Raphael or "Little Ireland" along Bluff, West Third and West Fourth Streets. In most cases, virtually nothing is known about the designers or builders of these houses. They are, to a large extent, the anonymous architecture of the working classes and were not noted by the newspapers when

West Fourth Street area

Nineteenth Street and Central Avenue

1215 Washington Street

1212 Elm Street

2955 Jackson Street

1221 University Avenue

1129-1131 White Street

40 Clarke Drive

built or torn down. They are not fully understood by architects and little appreciated by historians. Nevertheless, they are the most representative building type of Dubuque architecture.

To merely list a few examples of local "vernacular" buildings is perhaps sufficient to illustrate some of the different characteristics of this architectural style. Among earlier examples are houses at 1215 Washington Street, 1212 Elm Street, 471 - 473 and 489 - 491 West Fourth Street. An interesting group of houses with covered passageways into rear courts can be found at 1889-1915 Central. Outstanding one or one and one-half story houses include 1012 and 1016 Rhomberg and 504 Twenty-Second Street. Varied porch types can be seen on buildings at 1221 University and 2509 Broadway. Two well-proportioned double houses possessing totally different appearances are at 346 West Locust and 1129 - 1131 White while a fine row exists at 427 - 449 Summit. Other varied examples include the buildings at 40 Clarke Drive, 1543 Washington Street, 711 Twenty-Second Street and 2955 Jackson. The two houses at 1263 and 1267 Jackson represent an interesting contrast showing the visual effect different roof shapes can create. The houses at 1163, 1209, 1245 and 1295 Highland all possess outstanding porches as well as details taken from Greek Revival, Italian Villa, Queen Anne and other styles. Numerous other examples could be referred to. Such streets as Loras, Washington, Jackson, Rhomberg, University, Bluff, West Third, White and Central are lined with vernacular buildings constructed between the Civil War and the end of the Nineteenth Century.

504 Twenty-second Street

711 Twenty-second St.

346 West Locust Street

1543 Washington Street

2509 Broadway Street

Row houses at 427-449 Summit Street

1012 and 1016 Rhomberg (page 79)

1295 Highland Place

1267 Jackson Street

1163 Highland Place

1245 Highland Place

1209 Highland Place

Saint Mary's Church

Historical tradition tells us that Dubuque's Irish and German elements were not particularly known for their brotherly love of each other, so it is somewhat ironic that the German congregation hired John Mullany, the Irish architect who designed Saint Raphael's, to design a new church in 1864. Father Hoffmann reports in his *Centennial History of the Archdiocese of Dubuque* that:

> Mr. John Mullany of Dubuque was chosen architect for the new church . . . It has been said that he used the Cathedral of Salisbury as his working model. However, in all justice to the Salisbury Cathedral, it must be mentioned that the only resemblance of the new church to the old was the tower and a hybrid species of the florid Gothic style. The tower of Saint Mary's which rises 250 feet, is one of the finest spires in the Mississippi Valley.[6]

Other sources indicate the height of the spire as 236 feet, 243 feet and 252 feet, but whatever the actual measurement it probably does not really matter, because it is the tallest steeple in Dubuque by at least fifty feet. Saint Mary's was dedicated in 1867. When completed, the cost was $97,000 or more than $17,000 above the architect's estimate. The building is 169 feet long and 69 feet wide. Constructed of brick on a stone foundation, Saint Mary's German Catholic Church has been carefully preserved for over 100 years. Perhaps its most unique feature is the organ, built by the Hook Organ Company of Boston in 1870. The order for the instrument called for a three manual tracker action organ with thirty-three registers and twenty-six stops. Someone is said to have

Loras Academy (page 89)

First United Presbyterian Church

Saint John's Episcopal Church

penciled in the margin of the order book the note, "an organ like this west of the Mississippi in 1870?"[7] The instrument was rebuilt in 1965 and remains one of the finest instruments in any Dubuque church.

Saint Mary's church represents one of several local examples of High Victorian Gothic architecture, a style based on the earlier Gothic Revival style but with more emphasis on vertical proportion, variety of color and surface texture with strong scale contrasts between detail elements. While the early Gothic Revival was based on English models, the High Victorian Gothic borrowed from Italy, Germany and France as well. Other characteristics include complex roof lines and solid external woodwork used as framing instead of "gingerbread" trim. In the United States this style of architecture was primarily used for churches and educational buildings. Most examples were constructed between 1860 and 1880.

Saint John's Episcopal Church at Loras and Main represents another significant example of High Victorian Gothic building in Dubuque. Saint John's was constructed between 1875 and 1878, replacing a small brick church that had been built in 1851 at the corner of Ninth and Locust. The present church is constructed of limestone quarried near Farley. Its plan forms a cross, the traditional Anglican arrangement. The walls are rough, while windows, doors and banding courses are smooth.

Saint John's, and Saint Luke's Methodist Church, which will be discussed later, together contain eleven of

First Congregational Church

Robinson-Lacy house, 1640 Main Street (page 92)

the fourteen major Tiffany windows that are documented to exist in Iowa churches. The Congregational Church in Dubuque also has one Tiffany window while the other two are at Iowa City and Council Bluffs.[8] Saint John's has five major windows from the New York studios of Louis Tiffany. They are the two Peabody Memorial Windows, the Seymour Memorial Window, Coyningham Memorial Window, and the Daniels Memorial Window.

Other Dubuque churches in the High Victorian Gothic style are the First United Presbyterian Church at Seventeenth and Iowa and the First Congregational Church at Tenth and Locust. The United Presbyterian Church has an offset corner tower topped with an octagonal steeple. It is constructed of finely detailed brickwork with limestone trim and was completed during the 1880's. The Congregational Church at Tenth and Locust has a Tiffany memorial window and a thirteen-foot diameter rose window, the largest in Dubuque. It was designed by David Jones, a local architect. Construction began in 1857 but was not completed until 1860. The organ was installed in 1863. The memorial windows were installed during an 1895 remodeling. The interior of the First Congregational Church is finished with native walnut woodwork. The original church bell rang all night until it cracked while announcing Lee's surrender after the Civil War. In front of the church are two ornate cast iron street lamps, excellent examples of once-common Victorian street furniture.

One other group of High Victorian Gothic buildings should be mentioned. The former Loras Academy buildings on Loras Avenue are partially built in the style. Later additions are examples of Second Empire architecture. The original portions were constructed as early as 1854 for use as a marine hospital. In 1873 a school, Saint Joseph's College, was opened in them. New buildings were added in 1878, and further additions were made in 1882. These later additions were built in the Second Empire style and can be identified by their mansard roofs in contrast to the earlier gable-roofed portions with their pointed towers. Historically, the hospital that was located in this group of buildings was the first in Dubuque. It was operated by the Sisters of Charity, B.V.M. and was used by cholera victims during the epidemics of 1855-1858. Because of their scale and architectural variety, these buildings are significant. One of the most interesting scenes in Dubuque is the view looking down Loras Avenue from Alta Vista Street past the old Loras Academy buildings toward the town and river.

In contrast to the vertical emphasis of Dubuque's post Civil War Gothic architecture is another stylistic development of the same period that is usually referred to as High Victorian Italianate. This style also had many sources based upon Italian traditions tempered by French influences from the Baroque era of Louis XIV. It was best suited for domestic and commercial buildings. Unlike some of the major revival styles, no great architects propounded High Victorian Italianate archi-

1453-1455 Main Street

Bishop's Block

1257 Locust Street

324-326 West Locust Street

975 Locust Street

tecture as the solution to all building problems. Nevertheless, buildings constructed in this idiom are generally handsome, well proportioned and even somewhat dignified. Arched windows, two-story bays and bracketed cornices are basic features. Dubuque has several good examples including double houses at 1453-1455 Main, 1257 Locust and 324-326 West Locust. There is also an interesting row house built in the High Victorian Italianate style at 975 Locust. The old Bishop's Block at the corner of First and Main with its varied window treatment for each floor, bold cornice and capped corner turret represents an adaptation of the style to a commercial structure. The Bishop's Block once housed Walker and Company, a wholesale produce house and later was used by Western Grocery. In recent years the building has been a warehouse.

A singular local example of an interesting style is the present T. Ellsworth house at 1492 Locust. It was built in 1883 for Dubuque businessman Benjamin B. Richards, owner of a boot and shoe factory. The building's tall proportions, high, steep roofs and irregular silhouette are all characteristic of the Stick Style of architecture. Other features of the style include projecting eaves supported by large brackets, exposed framing in the gable end of a roof and varied wall surfaces usually framed with "stick-work" meant to suggest timber construction. When porches or verandas are present, they are usually large. The Richards house has seven fireplaces and is finished with seven different kinds of wood.

In its earliest manifestations the Stick Style probably owed something to the Swiss Chalet, but it has come to be regarded as one of the most purely American nineteenth century architectural developments.[9] The style flourished during the quarter century between 1850 and the Philadelphia Centennial Exposition of 1876. Like other domestic architectural developments of the nineteenth century, the Stick Style was popularized by pattern books containing different adaptations of the style. Some pattern books were reprinted several times, and prominent architects even designed elaborate Stick Style "cottages" at such places as Newport, Rhode Island, usually noted for more substantial houses designed in more impressive styles.

The Richards house is a noteworthy example of this somewhat unique style of architecture. It is also one of the very few Dubuque houses that has been occupied by members of the same family since it was built.

One of the predominant architectural styles to appear in Dubuque during the period between 1860 and 1890 was the Second Empire or Franco-American style. The universal hallmark of the style is the high mansard roof cut by dormer windows that often take different shapes even on the same building. The slope of the mansard roof could be straight, convex, concave or S-curved. Second Empire buildings appear tall and three dimensional. Decorative features were commonly used and included such elements as iron cresting on the roof, corner quoins, decorative moldings, bracketed eaves, belvederes and window panes of colored glass. Brick was the usual construction material although Dubuque has examples built of stone and wood as well.

The Second Empire style was used for residential, commercial, governmental and institutional structures. Few Second Empire churches were built, but many parsonages have mansard roofs. The style takes its name from the French Second Empire of Napoleon II. The concept of the mansard roof is attributed to a French architect of the seventeenth century, Francois Mansart who was seeking a solution to the functional problem of how to provide more light and more space in the top floor or attic of a building. The design solution proved to be both practical and aesthetically pleasing.

> The typical mansard house is handsome without and comfortable within. The best of them with their deep porches, tall French windows, massive cornices and sweeping roofs topped by iron cresting are buildings of striking power and dignity.[10]

Obviously a mansard roofed building cannot have less than two stories, and most have three or four. Second Empire buildings were very suitable to American building conditions during the 1860's and 1870's. A mansard roofed house looked equally elegant standing alone or as part of a connected row. Either way it could be as plain or as fancy as the builder desired.

Perhaps Dubuque's most noticed Second Empire house is the Robinson-Lacy home at 1640 Main. Architecturally, it displays all of the style's important charac-

1492 Locust Street

teristics and is certainly one of the most elegant houses in the city. With the exception of a second floor window that has been altered, the original architecture is well preserved. Among the most interesting exterior features are the window moldings, the ornate bracketed eaves and the unusually fine cast iron cresting along the roof. John R. Robinson, a prominent Dubuque attorney built the house in about 1878. His daughter married Judge Lacy, and the house remained in the Lacy family until 1936 when Alois M. Hoffmann purchased it and converted it into a funeral home.

Robinson built his house to last. There are reportedly 10,000 cubic feet of rock in the foundation, and the outside walls are twenty-six inches thick. The walls are double brick with a four inch air space between. The woodwork throughout is of solid mahogany and walnut that was custom carved in Boston and then shipped to Dubuque. There are two heating systems, one hot air and the other radiator steam heat. The house adjoins Jackson Park which was the first cemetery in Dubuque. When the city accepted the land for a park, the bodies were exhumed and moved to Linwood Cemetery.

Mary of the Angels home at Sixth and Bluff represents an interesting case study of the adaptability of Second Empire architecture. At first glance, Mary of the Angels home looks like one large structure but in reality it consists of a private home with three later additions.

The original portion of what is today Mary of the Angels home is the house that Dubuque architect F. D. Hyde designed for Jesse P. Farley in 1879. It cost $20,000 and was one of the finest residences in the city at the time. Farley's house had twelve rooms, plate glass windows and five ornate fireplaces including one of Vermont marble with onyx pillars inlaid with china enamel designs that cost over $500.00.

J. P. Farley house, Sixth and Bluff Streets

Mary of the Angels home, Sixth and Bluff Streets

701 Bluff Street

J. P. Farley settled at Dubuque in 1833 and became one of the thirteen wealthiest men in the city in 1857.[11] He served three consecutive terms as mayor and helped organize the Dubuque Insurance Company and Central Improvement Company. In 1876 he furnished capital to establish the Farley and Loetscher Company which was later to become the largest millwork firm in the world. One of Farley's main interests, however, was railroads. As early as 1853 he helped organize the Dubuque and Pacific Railway with Lucius Langworthy, General Jones and others. The town of Farley along its route is named for him. In 1873 when the Saint Paul and Pacific Railway was forced into receivership, partly as a result of a nationwide financial depression, Farley was appointed the reorganization manager. For the next seven years Farley spent much time in Saint Paul working to re-establish the line on firm financial footing. During the early 1890's the Saint Paul line became involved in a lawsuit against James J. Hill's Great Northern Railway. Farley lost the case over routes of the two lines but refused an offer by Hill to settle for one million dollars. Instead, he appealed the case to the United States Supreme Court hiring six of the nation's top attorneys to plead his case. One of them, George Edmond of Vermont, was paid $1,000 per hour for his services during one court appearance. In order to support his case Farley was forced to mortgage his factory and 600 acres of land he owned. After the Supreme Court ruled against him in 1892, Farley was forced to sell his house for $15,000 to the Sisters of Saint Francis to help pay his legal fees. He died two years later.

The Sisters of Saint Francis used the house as a boarding home for young women. In 1899 Dubuque architect Guido Beck designed an addition on the west side of the house. It contains twenty private rooms, kitchen and dining facilities and common rooms. Another addition in 1911 included a chapel, thirty-two rooms and other facilities. Several shacks that had been built in the 1830's behind the house were torn down in 1916. The south wing of the present building, containing thirty-six rooms and new dining facilities, was added in 1929. Both the 1911 and 1929 additions were designed by Fridolin Heer and son. Although the last addition was not completed until nearly fifty years after Farley built the original portion as his house, all of the additions carry through the original Second Empire design motifs right down to the window moldings and bracketed eaves. This building, and its neighbors along Bluff Street between Sixth and Seventh, form one of the most interesting street frontages in Dubuque. Of particular interest is the double house at 701 Bluff that is viewed down Seventh Street. It was designed by Thomas T. Carkeek for Dubuque businessman George W. Healey.

Along with the Robinson-Lacy house, one of the city's most prominent Second Empire homes is the present Behr Funeral Home at 1491 Main. It was designed by Fridolin Heer during the 1870's for Alexander Young. Constructed entirely of stone, the house stands solid and dignified. The exceptional craftsmanship exhibited in its construction illustrates the talents of Dubuque

1651 White Street

1491 Main Street

stonecutters at their peak. The panels on the north wall are especially interesting.

One of the few Second Empire houses in Dubuque with a belvedere is the structure at 1651 White Street. Its peculiar shape has made this structure a neighborhood landmark.

Following the national trend, Second Empire religious architecture is rare in Dubuque. There are no local churches in the style, but the parish rectories for Saint Raphael's and Saint Mary's are good examples of Second Empire design as is the older portion of Saint Columbkille's School on Rush Street. The Saint Francis convent and Immaculate Conception school buildings on Davis Street are some of the largest and most imposing Second Empire structures in the city. Other large buildings include Bethany home on Lincoln and the apartments at 1100 - 1150 Main Street. The original portion of Bethany Home was the Christian Loetscher family residence. Among many other Second Empire houses are those at 652 Needham Place, the H. Scott house at 788 Fenelon Place, 563 West Eleventh Street, 1611 Main, 1631-33 Main, 1655 Main, 1450 Iowa, 1552 Locust and 489 Loras. There are also examples of double houses and apartments in the Second Empire style along Clarke Drive, Rhomberg, Central, Jackson, Washington and White streets.

A final monument of Second Empire architecture in Dubuque is the present town clock designed in 1873 by Fridolin Heer to replace the original clock that had collapsed the previous year killing three people. The

788 Fenelon Place

1631-1633 Main Street

Immaculate Conception School

563 West Eleventh Street

Bethany Home, 1005 Lincoln Avenue

1100-1150 Main Street

652 Needham Place

1611 Main Street

new clock is built with heavy stone caps and lintels and is three stories high. The clockworks were manufactured by Howard & Company of Boston and cost $5,309. Originally it operated by means of weights running up and down a shaft. The mechanism was wound daily by two boys who spent an hour and a half at the task. About 1900 a motor was installed to wind the clock. In 1971 Dubuque's town clock was moved from its location on a building between Eighth and Ninth Streets to a pedestal in the intersection of Seventh and Main providing a major focal point for the downtown urban renewal and pedestrianway project.

Queen Anne Houses and the Emergence of Modern Styles

Dubuque's post Civil War growth was interrupted in 1873 by a nationwide financial panic caused by stock speculation, over expansion of western agricultural lands, a world-wide drop in prices and the general collapse of a period of corruption that was unparalleled in American history. The depression lasted for about three years until the 1876 U.S. Centennial Exposition at Philadelphia captured the country's attention and signaled a new interest in American idealism. Thousands of people from all over the country visited Philadelphia in 1876, and one of the things that was most noticed was the half-timbered buildings the British government had erected to house their staff. A popular building magazine of the time enthusiastically described the British houses and further noted:

> But the chief thing that will strike the observant eye in this style is its wonderful adaptability to this country,

> not to the towns indeed, but to the land at large . . . It is to be hoped that the next millionaire who puts up a cottage at Long Branch will have a house ample enough to entertain a Prince, yet exceedingly cozy, cool in summer, and yet abundantly warm in winter, plain enough and yet capable of the highest ornamental development.[12]

Many names, including Queen Anne, Neo-Jacobean, Free Classic and Modern American Renaissance, have been given to this type of house. The style originally developed in England using Elizabethan motifs such as half-timber construction. Its appearance in America is said to represent a reaction against High Victorian architectural "reality" and a renewed interest in a picturesque past appealing to a country that had lost much of its confidence during the Panic of 1873.[13]

The primary architectural characteristic of a Queen Anne house is the irregularity of plan and massing. Roofs are high and multiple, with ridges meeting at right angles. Upper stories may project beyond the lower. Round or polygonal towers and turrets are common, and elaborate chimneys are often major design elements. Large porches are almost standard features that contribute to the overall appearance of the building. A variety of construction materials appears on the same structure. It is not unusual to see brick used on the lower floor, shingling on the upper stories and half timbering in a gable. Bay windows are common, and other windows take almost any shape except the Gothic pointed arch. Ornament is lavishly applied but tends to be small in scale.

The overall appearance of a Queen Anne house might be called ghastly by any modern standard, but shrewd observers have noted that such picturesque houses:

> often provided entertainment for the passerby and, for the occupant, surprises, places for children to hide, crannies, inglenooks, attics, dramatic balconies, ceremonial staircases with railing to slide down, space, carved wood and colored glass. They were untidy but they could provide joyous human habitat.[14]

Although Queen Anne houses were being built in the U.S. during the 1870's the style did not become fully developed in the Midwest until the late 1880's and 1890's. The majority of Dubuque houses constructed in this style probably date from the decade between 1885 and 1895. A few may have been built as late as the first decade of the twentieth century.

It would be difficult for anyone who has walked or driven up Locust Street to have missed noticing the two houses next to the Masonic Temple at Eleventh and Locust. The large stone house at 1105 Locust was built by F. D. Stout and will be discussed later. Next door at 1145 Locust is the house H. L. Stout built for his daughter Fannie. It is the most elaborate example of Queen Anne architecture ever built in Dubuque and, as such, is nearly impossible to describe in simple terms. Combined in a frenzy of the architect's imagination are elements of Greek Revival, Gothic, Romanesque, Oriental, Byzantine and Richardsonian architecture. It was designed about 1892 by Fridolin Heer of Dubuque. In looking at this house, one's attention is drawn to the complex configuration of the roof and the massive Byzantine-domed tower on the corner. A closer look, however, reveals a multitude of details as unique as the house itself. The molded cornices of the porches, geometrical brickwork on the chimney, slate roof on the dome, varied porch railings, leaded windows and wooden ornament on the roof are all worthy of note. Although the house was converted to a funeral home some years ago, both the interior woodwork and exterior appearance have been carefully preserved.

The Stouts were an important lumbering family of Dubuque who had extensive holdings in Wisconsin and the West. They also participated in horse racing, and the Stout Stables owned the famous Dubuque race horse "Nutwood", sire of 120 record setting trotters and twenty-five pacers. A track that once attracted thousands to regular horse races was located at the north end of Dubuque.

The H. L. Stout house may be unique to the architectural history of Dubuque but it is not the city's only elaborate example of the Queen Anne style. The present Quinlan Chiropractic office at 1337 Main is an interesting study of changing personal tastes reflected in the architectural embellishment of one's home. As far as is known, First National Bank President Charles H. Eighmey built this house in the early 1890's. Eighmey had come to Dubuque from upstate New York in 1850. He practiced law until 1870 when he joined the bank. He was also a trustee of Saint Luke's Methodist Episcopal Church and was instrumental in promoting the construction of the congregation's present church. Shortly after it was completed, one contemporary account described Eighmey's house:

> Their house is a palatial residence, tastefully and richly furnished, and the interior furnishings are all of hard wood. It is one of the most beautiful homes of the city and in it Mr. Eighmey takes great delight.[15]

As originally constructed, the C. H. Eighmey house was a straightforward interpretation of Queen Anne design. The distinguishing features were the two asymmetrical towers at either side of the facade. The smaller tower is topped by a pointed cap while the larger has a domed metal roof. A dramatic alteration occurred as the result of an early twentieth century remodeling. At this time the overwhelming Greek Revival portico and gable were added giving the house its present appearance. Needless to say, it is somewhat surprising to encounter the formal elegance of a Greek temple flanked by two picturesque towers. The overall experience is very visual! The architectural reasoning behind the Greek Revival additions can probably be traced to the Neo-Classical Revival movement around the turn of the century. Several Dubuque structures from this period will be considered separately.

"Redstone", the only remaining Cooper family house represents another interpretation of the Queen

1337 Main Street (as built)

3000 Central Avenue

1337 Main Street

581 Clarke Drive

3087 Central Avenue

2735 Windsor Avenue

Anne style. It was constructed about 1890 at the corner of Fifth and Bluff and is built of red brick with matched sandstone trim. Thomas T. Carkeek of Dubuque was the architect. The dominant architectural features are the large Romanesque tower, fine stained glass windows and the ornamental stonework below the gables and around the entry porches. "Redstone" was originally one of three houses built by the August A. Cooper family. Cooper was another one of Dubuque's early settlers who engaged in a number of business enterprises but became known as the most famous wagon maker in the west. For many years the Cooper Wagon Works was one of the city's largest employers.

One of Dubuque's earliest Queen Anne houses is at 581 Clarke Drive. Dr. Ernest M. Porter began building this residence in 1872, but the Depression of 1873 halted completion until 1875. Porter was a local dentist and racing enthusiast whose horse "Major" was a well known harness racer. He occupied the house until his death in 1887. It then passed through the hands of many owners but has remained in good condition after 100 years. Built of wood, the structure's most unusual architectural element is the highly picturesque entrance tower with its multiple roofs and hooded windows. A wing on the side was added around the turn of the century by a later owner. The house sits well back on an attractively landscaped lot.

After the unique local "vernacular" style, Queen Anne houses are probably the second most common style of residential architecture in Dubuque. Indeed, in many

"Redstone", Fifth and Bluff Streets (page 101)

H. L. Stout house, 1145 Locust Street (page 100)

1921 Madison Street

1133 Highland Place

1105 Grove Terrace

examples, such as the houses at 3000 and 3087 Central and the Linwood Cemetery office at 2735 Windsor, both local vernacular and Queen Anne elements are combined in imaginative and visually interesting ways. Various interpretations of the Queen Anne style in wood can be seen in houses at 900 West Third, 1105 Grove Terrace, and 1921 Madison. The houses on Grove Terrace and West Third Street illustrate the common Queen Anne building practice of using imbricated or patterned shingling. Both houses also portray many of the style's architectural cliches. The house on Madison Street was owned by a Dubuque jeweler and watchmaker during the 1890's and is a classic of Queen Anne design. Notable features include the spindlework on the porches, the corner window treatment and the well-proportioned corner turret. This house also has one of the most spectacular settings in all of Dubuque.

Yet another interpretation of Queen Anne architecture can be seen in the house at 1025 Walnut Street. Here a mansard roof is combined with a cube-like corner tower and third-floor balcony. The main porch also displays some outstanding Victorian spindlework. Almost as unusual is another residence at 1133 Highland Place that possesses characteristics of both Italian Villa and Queen Anne design. Finally, the contrasting effects that can be achieved through the use of varied materials is evident in Queen Anne style residences at 1045 West Third Street and at the corner of Loras and Main. Both houses are basically similar in plan but appear strikingly different. The house on West Third is built of red brick and sandstone according to "traditional" Queen Anne concepts. It appears to be staid and dignified. Interesting architectural details include Palladian windows in the gables and leaded glass in the corner turret, ornamental stone and brickwork and classical columns in matched pairs around the broad porch. The house on Main is constructed of gray brick contrasted by geometrically-laid pattern brick and green tile roofs. The porch that sweeps across both the front and side of the house is supported by massive square-stone columns with decorative panels on the four sides. The corner tower is six-sided and exhibits exceptional ornamental brickwork. The classically-proportioned gable facing Main Street contains an elaborate Palladian window.

1045 West Third Street

Loras Boulevard and Main Street

Dubuque County Court House and Town Clock
(page 116)

1025 Walnut Street (page 107)

Queen Anne residences of almost every description continued to be erected in Dubuque throughout the 1890's and even into the early twentieth century. For a time during the early nineties, the style was so popular that some people added peaked turrets to their earlier houses or otherwise remodeled them along "modern" Queen Anne lines. After World War II these fussy Victorian houses were no longer fashionable, and many owners cut down the turrets and ripped off the porches or other fussy ornament. A large number were also covered with metal siding, again in the name of modernization. Only recently has there been a renewed interest in these most picturesque examples of Victorian architectural design. Imaginative residents are discovering that Queen Anne houses offer an interesting as well as practical living environment in terms of spatial arrangements and features that cannot be found in most mid-twentieth century homes.

Even as the Queen Anne style was reaching the peak of its popularity in Dubuque around 1890, other architectural developments were making inroads into local buildings practices. The revivalist movements based on European and classical models did not die out completely until well into the twentieth century, but there was increasing interest in a number of stylistic developments that were created by American architects. The years 1892 and 1893 were a turning point. The Columbian Exposition at Chicago and the Depression of 1893 set the stage for a period of architectural eclecticism that lasted until the stock market crash of 1929 and the Great Depression of the 1930's. It was during this era around the turn of the century that modern American architecture emerged from the tangle of Gothic, Romanesque, Neo-Classical, Italianate, Georgian and Queen Anne styles. As illustrated by the many different types of buildings erected between 1890 and 1930, Dubuque was caught up in the architectural frenzy of the time.

A Century of Dubuque Architecture

The Later Years, 1890-1930

The Later Years, 1890-1930

A Period of Transition

By 1890 Iowa was emerging as one of the leading agricultural states. At the same time, a diversified industrial base was being developed. Dubuque had already established its reputation as a commercial and industrial center with sawmilling, meat packing, brewing, railroading and various manufacturing operations all prospering. The Mississippi River continued to be important to Dubuque as the means of transporting many local products. The city's gas, water and electric utilities had all been established by 1890, and the street railway system, in operation since 1867, was electrified in that year. The streetcars continued to run until their replacement by buses in 1928. The completion of the Grand Opera House in 1890 marked the beginning of Dubuque's theatrical heyday. In 1890 the unique Fenelon Place Elevator was already eight years old and had been rebuilt once after a fire in 1884. It was to burn again in 1892 before being reconstructed in its present form. The elevator was originally constructed by Dubuque banker, J. K. Graves, for quick transportation home at noon but soon became a public conveyance for residents living above the bluff with the fare remaining at just five cents until 1962. In addition to the regular daily customers more than 150,000 visitors ride the cable car each year making it Dubuque's most popular tourist attraction. Although not an architectural landmark, the

Fenelon Place Elevator (1880's)

Fenelon Place Elevator is one of Dubuque's most unusual historical attractions.

During the 1870's and 1880's much of Dubuque's present architectural character was created as most of the buildings designed in the revivalist styles already discussed were constructed. Perhaps more important than different styles in establishing the city's character, were the unifying elements of similar scale, mass, color and materials found on hundreds of local buildings. For example, a coherent commercial streetscape of this period can still be viewed along portions of Main Street and Central Avenue despite the visual chaos of mid-twentieth century signs and "modernization" of storefronts. In a like manner, many residential districts, when viewed from a bluff top vantage point, appear unified in scale and character punctuated only by the spires of neighborhood churches.

The creation of Dubuque's visual character was not, however, the conscious result of any master plan. For the most part, each architect and builder worked independently within the minimal confines of whatever public safety and other codes existed at the time. The mere diversity of architectural styles that appeared after the Civil War suggest an independent approach to design, while the nature of available materials, construction technology, economics and the size of most city lots produced constraints that resulted in similarities of building scale. This was particularly true insofar as height was concerned. A four or five story structure was about as high as could be effectively served using only stairways.

In contrast to the seventies and eighties, the decade of the 1890's produced a number of building innovations that changed the course of American architecture away from European models based on centuries of tradition, toward new expressions of American individualism. The use of iron and steel as major structural elements allowed new architectural freedom. The perfection of mechanical elevators and the development of new construction techniques all but eliminated height restrictions, resulting in the creation of "skyscraper" commercial and office buildings. Improvements in lighting, heating and ventilating and the development of modern fireproof construction also influenced the way in which buildings of all types were erected. Dubuque was not isolated from these changes in building technology. Many structures built between 1890 and the outbreak of World War I represent local adaptations of national trends. At the same time, however, it is important to note that there was not a sudden break with historical building traditions. In fact, modern technological improvements were often incorporated into traditional architectural designs. Nineteenth century stylistic developments lasted well into the twentieth century.

In 1884 the Sacred Heart parish hired Dubuque architect Fridolin Heer to design a new and larger church. The parish consisted of persons from the German speaking districts of Europe including Bavaria, Tyrol,

Sacred Heart Catholic Church

Switzerland, Alsace-Lorraine, Luxemburg, the Rhineland, Baden, Westphalia, Hanover, Saxony and Silesia. Sacred Heart parish was formed in 1879 by subdividing Saint Mary's congregation. The first church was completed in 1880 at a cost of $5,500 and is presently used for the Sacred Heart School. It was also designed by Heer. Actual work on the new church at 635 East 22nd Street began in 1885. The corner stone was laid in 1887 and the building was completed the following year. Built of brick, the 63 by 160 foot building can seat over 1,000 people. Its two towers are 135 and 200 feet high. Heer's design for Sacred Heart church marks a somewhat late appearance in Dubuque of the Romanesque Revival style. This style originated in Germany and spread to the United States during the 1850's and 1860's. It was especially popular for churches and public buildings.

The most prominent features of Sacred Heart church are its two unequal towers, almost a universal characteristic of churches designed in the Romanesque Revival style. Another key feature is the use of round arches for all door and window openings. The round arch is usually repeated in miniature along the gable and can be seen on the facade of Sacred Heart church. Romanesque Revival structures are generally symmetrical, and wall surfaces are broad and smooth. In contrast to the Gothic style, buttresses are nearly flush against the building walls. Round wheel or rose windows are actually Gothic in origin but can be found in many Romanesque churches.

Holy Trinity Catholic Church

Villa Raphael

There are at least two other Romanesque Revival religious structures in Dubuque. Villa Raphael on Mount Loretta and Holy Trinity Catholic Church on Rhomberg Avenue were built in 1909 and 1910 respectively. Villa Raphael was used as a motherhouse by the Sisters of the Presentation and is now a home for retired priests. It is an imposing four-story building flanked by hexagonal towers. A cupola rises from the center of the roof. Five three-story arches contain double windows on each floor, and a classical portico looms over the entrance. The pyramidal roofs on the towers and cupola are frequently used on Romanesque structures. Holy Trinity Church was completed at a cost of over $47,000. It boasts many traditional characteristics of the style. Of particular interest, again, are the towers as compared to both Sacred Heart church and Villa Raphael.

The firm of Fridolin Heer and Son was also called upon to design a new county court house in 1891 to replace the run-down structure built in 1839. The building they produced is the city's only example of Beaux Arts Classicism architecture and ranks with the Town Clock as one of the two most prominent landmarks in downtown Dubuque.

Many public and quasi-public buildings from libraries to railroad stations and courthouses were designed in the Beaux Arts Classicism style. The monumental aspects of this architecture were appropriate for the affluence of the era.

> Immense pride and superlative artisanship in both interior and exterior details were mandatory to merit the respect and honor of the citizens.[1]

The Dubuque County Court House is 88 by 125 feet in size. Its center tower is 190 feet high and is topped by a fourteen-foot bronze statue of justice. Other allegorical figures of laminated pewter appear at different places on the building. Four large statues of winged angels with trumpets were removed during World War I and melted down to aid the war effort. They originally stood at the four corners of the square base of the tower. Built of gray Indiana limestone, brick and molded terra cotta, the structure illustrates the best of Beaux Arts Classicism design. The structure's mass, complex roof configuration, arched openings and monumental steps are all typical elements of the style. The use of figure sculpture and molded relief is also common. Originally, the Court House had a slate roof, and there was a stained glass dome on the fourth floor that was removed when the elevator was installed. Carved oak woodwork is still visible throughout the interior. In recent years there has been much controversy over the continued use of the Dubuque County Court House, but its preservation seems assured. It was one of the first local buildings listed in the National Register of Historic Places. A state historical preservation grant of $35,000 was awarded to undertake exterior repairs, and further renovation work has been proposed.

The work of a man who never saw Dubuque had a profound impact on the design of some of the city's most important landmark structures. Henry Hobson Richardson, along with Louis Sullivan and Frank Lloyd Wright, is often considered one of the three greatest American-born architects. Richardson only lived forty years, and all of his designs were constructed during the last fifteen years of his life. Beginning with his design for Boston's Trinity Church in 1872, the homes, churches, court houses, railroad stations, libraries, warehouses and other buildings he created completely changed the American concept of Romanesque architecture. His work had such an impact that the name Richardsonian is often given to his interpretation of the Romanesque style.

Like the Romanesque Revival style, Richardsonian Romanesque design emphasizes use of the rounded arch. Rough cut stone is the usual construction material, but brick with contrasting trim is also used. In public and commercial buildings, two to four stories are sometimes grouped behind a single arched opening. Chimneys are squat, heavy set and plain. Tall square towers are topped with pyramidal roofs, while the polygonal turrets at building corners have conical roofs. Richardsonian Romanesque buildings appear heavy and massive to most observers. The large scale of many such buildings emphasizes this appearance.

Dubuque has several Richardsonian Romanesque buildings, each representing a different interpretation of the style. Central High School at Fifteenth and Locust is one of the best local examples. Built of Wisconsin sandstone, this 92 by 104 foot structure embodies many characteristics of the style. Notable features include the coarse stonework, massive arches, high roofs and tall clock tower. The interior is finished with maple and oak woodwork. When the new school was completed in 1895,

Central High School

the Dubuque *Daily Herald* noted that it was provided with every modern convenience.

> It is a temple of learning indeed, and its superior, we might without fear of contradiction say, its equal does not exist in Iowa. Like everything else she undertakes, Dubuque can well be proud of her High School and the Dubuque men who built it.[2]

But it was the building's ventilation system that received the most attention at the grand opening.

> The ventilation on the first and second stories attracted great attention. A large fan operated by a dynamo in the basement draws in the pure outside air and forces it through pipes into the rooms giving the air in them a greater pressure than that outside, the result being that instead of air from outside coming in at the window cracks, the air inside seeks these means of escape and pneumonia breeding draughts are impossible. Other pipes about the room, into which the air is sucked, carry off the impure atmosphere and give a constant change.[3]

The Dubuque Central High School was designed by G. S. Mansfield of Freeport, Illinois. Six other architects, including F. Heer, T. T. Carkeek and G. Guilbert of Dubuque, competed for the commission. Heer was the leading local contender but lost the job on a four to two vote of the School Board. The reason Heer lost was that his recently completed Dubuque County Court House cost more than his estimate. Apparently the School Board overlooked the fact that at the time he was chosen architect of the new school, Mansfield was involved in a dispute over construction of the Clinton County Court House he had designed. The foundation alone cost more than double his $35,000 estimate.[4] The papers do not record whether the school was completed within the architect's cost estimate.

Saint Luke's United Methodist Church was completed in 1897 at a cost of over $100,000. Constructed of grey Indiana limestone, the present church is the successor to Iowa's first church, a small log structure that was erected in 1834. Although thoroughly Richardsonian Romanesque in concept, architect George Kramer's choice and handling of material makes his design appear more subdued than the high school. For example, exterior detail is very plain.

Architecturally, the church's windows are its most notable features. Saint Luke's contains more authenticated glass from the New York studio of Louis Tiffany than any other church in Iowa.[5] Every window is of Tiffany Favrile glass. Major pieces include the Cooley, Richardson, Hancock, Staples and Farley memorial windows. The Cooley window entitled "The Good Shepherd" was exhibited by the Tiffany Company at the Chicago Columbian Exposition in 1893 as their finest production.[6] It was later purchased for Saint Luke's. The visitor to Saint Luke's is likely to be awed by the beauty of the windows but should not overlook the Tiffany chandeliers, the brass altar railing, or the oak woodwork by the Farley and Loetscher Company of Dubuque. In addition to creating the windows, the Tiffany Company also had the contract for interior decorating and frescoing. The eighty-six foot high tower contains eleven bells that were installed in 1913. Like most other Dubuque

Saint Luke's United Methodist Church

churches, Saint Luke's has been maintained in excellent condition.

For over 130 years brewing has been an important local industry. Prior to 1900 eight breweries had been constructed in the city. The earliest breweries were built too long ago to be remembered by any living Dubuquer, but the beer gardens of nineeteenth-century Dubuque were an integral part of the city's way of life.

Iowa's last operating brewery is at Dubuque. The Star Brewery still produces both Dubuque Star and Pickett's Premium beers. The riverfront building near the shot tower that houses the brewery is a good example of Romanesque industrial architecture. Its rounded arches, hanging turret over the entrance, ornamental brickwork and towering size have made this structure a Dubuque landmark for over eighty years.

Dubuque Star Brewery

Of all the breweries that have been constructed in Dubuque, however, none can match the Dubuque Brewing and Malting Company at 3000 Jackson Street. The five and seven story complex covers three acres and is the single most important piece of industrial architecture in Dubuque. The brewery represents an adaptation of the Richardsonian Romanesque style to meet the needs of a specialized industrial operation. Both in its overall conception and in the careful execution of the smallest detail, the brewery is superb. The architect was Louis Lehle of Chicago, perhaps the foremost brewery architect of the time. Fridolin Heer of Dubuque supervised the construction. Work began in 1894 and was completed

Dubuque Brewing and Malting Company

one year later by a crew of nearly 100 men. Some of the materials used included 89,000 cubic feet of stone for foundations, 25,000 cubic feet of concrete, 3.5 million brick, 5,000 square feet of cut stone and 800 square feet of iron. The cost was $500,000.

When opened, the Dubuque Brewing and Malting Company was one of the largest and most modern in the United States. Its annual production was 300,000 barrels. Anton Heeb, Adam Glab, Titus Schmid, M. Tschirgi and J. Schwind were the founders of the company that was a consolidation of their individual brewing interests. A guidebook published when the new brewery opened described their bold undertaking:

> It was designed with careful consideration of all the possibilities of the future by the best brewery engineering experts in the country. The latest machinery and most approved methods were installed; ice making machines, to be used exclusively for all cooling purposes, and the latest devices for bottling and marketing the product were put in, and everything that a thoroughly practical knowledge of the business could suggest has been added to the equipment.[7]

Colorful horse-drawn wagons delivered the beer to local outlets until after the turn of the century. Later a fleet of battery powered electric trucks were used. They were the first such vehicles in Iowa and could carry five tons. Between battery charges each truck could run thirty miles at a speed of six miles per hour and could negotiate ten percent grades.

After being shut down by Prohibition, the company never recovered. Attempts were made to reopen but

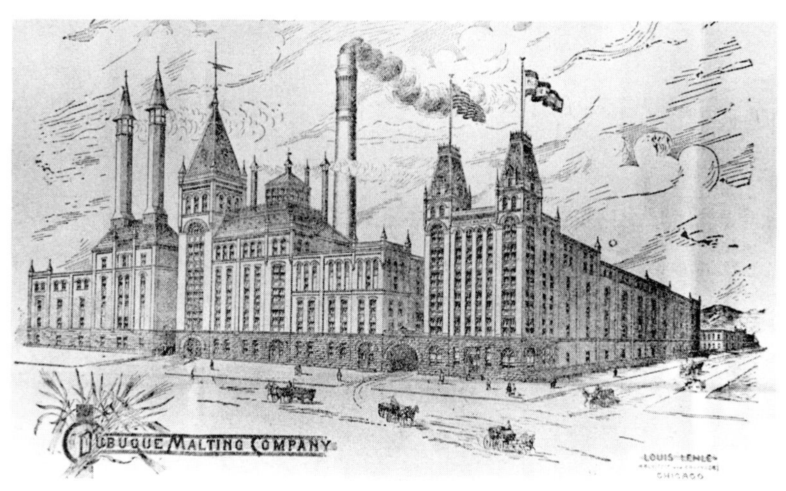

Architect's sketch, Dubuque Brewing and Malting Company

failed, and for a time a packing plant occupied the buildings. Since 1940 they have been used for warehouse purposes.

It has been said that historians, architects and others have ignored old breweries. This is unfortunately true. As expressed by the towering Richardsonian Romanesque shapes of the Dubuque Brewing and Malting Company buildings, the brewing industry has furnished some of this country's most distinctive industrial architecture. The industry itself has made important contributions to pasteurization and refrigeration processes now widely used in food preparation. During the nineteenth century when hundreds of family breweries flourished, beer was regarded as a mild and healthful beverage often recommended to replace stronger drinks. Brewing was a highly respected industry.

Mount Carmel Motherhouse

Another local example of Richardsonian Romanesque architecture is the Mount Carmel Motherhouse located at the southern end of Grandview Avenue. It was designed by John J. Egan of Chicago. The site commands one of the most impressive Mississippi River views of any place in Dubuque. At the time of its construction in 1893-1894 Mount Carmel was the largest convent in North America. The main wing is 240 feet long, seventy-six feet wide and thirty-five feet high, just slightly smaller than the Cathedral of Saint Raphael. It is built of brick with Bedfordstone trim. The interior is finished throughout with maple and oak woodwork. A major interior feature is the art gallery with its arched ceiling of cut stone. The total construction cost was $300,000.

At the time the new Motherhouse was constructed, the Sisters of Charity, BVM, operated schools and missions in Illinois, Wisconsin, Missouri, Kansas, Colorado, Nebraska, California and Iowa.

Odd Fellows Temple

Dubuque's only Richardsonian Romanesque house was built by lumberman F. D. Stout at 1105 Locust Street in 1890-1891. It reportedly cost over $300,000 to construct. Significant architectural elements include the building's massive appearance, rounded arches over doors and windows, leaded glass windows and very ornate interior. Of interest is the manner in which the hexagonal tower with its pointed roof is incorporated into the basically rectangular structure. While red sandstone is used exclusively for the exterior, the interior is finished in mahogany and rosewood. There are great onyx columns supporting the double doors between main rooms, and the original bathroom fixtures were of German silver.

In 1911 the Archdiocese of Dubuque bought the house from J. J. Nagle who had purchased it a few years earlier for a fraction of its original cost. It is probably fortunate that the Archdiocese acquired this house. They have maintained it in excellent condition, while other groups interested in purchasing it in 1911 had proposed various plans for demolishing the interior to make meeting rooms, apartments or clubrooms.[8]

Compared to the somewhat monumental structures we have been discussing, the old Odd Fellows Temple at Ninth and Locust may seem insignificant but illustrates an adaptation of the Richardsonian Romanesque style to conditions involving different materials and smaller scale construction. It is built of brick. The Odd Fellows building, in addition to its multi-storied arches, boasts a three-story hexagonal corner turret topped by one of Dubuque's finest weathervanes. Now used for offices and called the American Tower Building, the Odd Fellows Temple was designed in 1892 by Thomas T. Carkeek of Dubuque. With the exception of being painted black, its architectural character has been well preserved.

Rising land values and construction costs during the late nineteenth century increased the interest of both architects and developers in taller buildings. The solu-

F. D. Stout house, 1105 Locust

tion of structural problems and the development of elevators made high rise buildings technically practical, but the aesthetic problem of giving architectural unity to the tall facades remained unresolved until Chicago architect Louis Sullivan designed the Wainwright Building at St. Louis in 1890. Sullivan's solution was to create a simple form terminated by a flat roof and boldly projecting cornice. Other characteristics of the so-called Sullivanesque style include arched doorways and molded terra cotta or plaster relief ornament on cornices, doorways, window lintels and almost anyplace else the architect chose.

Both the present Stampfer and Fischer Buildings in downtown Dubuque exhibit Sullivanesque architectural characteristics. The Stampfer Building was originally called the Security Building and was constructed in 1896 by J. F. Stampfer and F. W. Altman. In recent years much of the present Fischer Building's architectural ornament has been removed or covered during remodeling projects, but some of the rich Sullivanesque detail is still visible on the upper stories. Upon its completion, the Bank and Insurance Building, as the structure was known during the 1890's, was described as the largest and most elegantly equipped business structure in the State of Iowa.

As the 1890's drew to a close, so did the Victorian age of architecture. Changing personal tastes and economic considerations effectively brought to an end the frantic development of revivalist styles that had characterized American architecture since before the Civil War. At the same time, a generation of American born and inspired master architects began to alter the course of American building. To be sure there were attempts to return once again to the classical models, but the new styles that emerged after 1900 were essentially American in concept. In general, the period between about 1890 and 1910 witnessed the division between modern American design and the historical traditions of the past.[9] The legacy of the Victorian architects, however, was far more than the mere creation of picturesque structural shapes. From a practical viewpoint, most of the conveniences associated with modern heating, cooking, lighting, and plumbing were introduced during the Victorian period.

> American Victorian homes were the first to have central heating by warm air furnaces, hot and cold running water, bathrooms, cooking ranges and indoor toilets. They also boasted high rooms, a big kitchen, both front and back yard and ample storage space in cellar and attic.[10]

It is significant to note that some of these modern improvements originated in Dubuque. The A. Y. McDonald Company, in particular, pioneered the development of plumbing apparatus that enabled running water and indoor bathrooms to be easily installed in houses of all types. Other local firms manufactured stoves and heating systems.

Architectural Developments After 1900

One of the unique aspects of Dubuque history has been the tradition of support for the performing arts

Security Building

Bank and Insurance Building

Fischer Building

Eagle Point Park Pavilion (page 142)

that dates from the first decades of settlement. A survey of theater buildings in Dubuque from 1837 to 1900 shows twenty-one separate theater locations. Fourteen of these theaters were spaces in buildings designed for other than theatrical purposes, and the remaining seven locations were buildings constructed primarily for theater use.

The fourteen theaters in other buildings included:

1. The Shakespeare Hall (1837 - ?)
2. The John S. Potter Theater (1839)
3. Terry's Saloon (1847)
4. Waples House (1848)
5. The Globe Hall (1850 - 1897?)
6. Lorimier Hall (1855 - 1876)
7. The St. Cloud Opera House (1857)
8. The Julien Theater (1856 - 1870)
9. The City Hall Theater (1857 - 1872)
10. The People's Theater (1857 - 1859)
11. First Turner Hall (1857)
12. Second Turner Hall (1860 - 1866)
13. No Turner Hall (1866 - 1872)
14. Third Turner Hall (1872 - 1967)

The seven separate theater buildings included:

1. Atheneum (1869 - 1877)
2. Duncan-Waller Opera House (1877 - 1892) (changed names several times)
3. Majestic (Orpheum) (1910 - present)
4. Standard Theater (1884 - ?)
5. Grand Opera House (1889 - present)
6. Stout Auditorium (1895 - present)
7. Saengerbund Auditorium (1896 - ?)

The site of the present Orpheum has seen theatrical operation since 1840, making it the oldest location in Iowa to have been continuously occupied by a theater, opera house, vaudeville or public entertainment house. When it was completed, the Majestic, or present Orpheum, was considered one of the finest theaters in the state of Iowa. It is the earliest known theater designed by C. W. and George L. Rapp who went on to become the nation's leading theater designers throughout the great entertainment era of the 1920's. Their work includes at least sixty of the most outstanding theaters built between 1910 and the Great Depression.

The design of a theater building was often dictated by the technical requirements for stairways, ceilings, seating, acoustics and stage rigging facilities. Architecturally, the Orpheum is an early twentieth-century adaptation of Second Empire style. The building's facade with its mansard roof and dormer windows is characteristically French, but some of the carved and molded detail suggests Italian Second Renaissance Revival influence. The architects were, in fact, said to have been inspired by a Paris Theater for their design. In its interior concept the Orpheum represents a transitional stage of theater design.

In the late nineteenth and early twentieth centuries, new ideas in dramatic presentation effectively rendered the Victorian playhouse obsolete. Early nineteenth century drama was presented in a manner that descended directly from the Shakespearean stage. Actors performed before a backdrop that suggested the setting. The thea-

Dubuque Theater Locations 1837 - 1900

1. City Hall – 1879
2. Turner Hall – 1859
3. Harmony Hall – 1880
4. St. Cloud Opera House – 1857
5. Stout Auditorium – 1895
6. Turner Halls
7. Grand Opera House – 1890
8. The Odeon – 1858
9. Odd Fellows Hall – 1867
10. Peoples Theater – 1857
11. The Standard – 1879
12. Globe Hall – 1855
13. The Julien – 1856
14. Athenaeum – 1840
    Opera House – 1877
    Bartels – 1896
    Coates Opera House – 1904
    Old Bijou – 1904
    New Bijou – 1909
    Majestic – 1911
    Orpheum – 1913
15. Shakespeare Hall – 1837
16. Varieties Theater – 1855

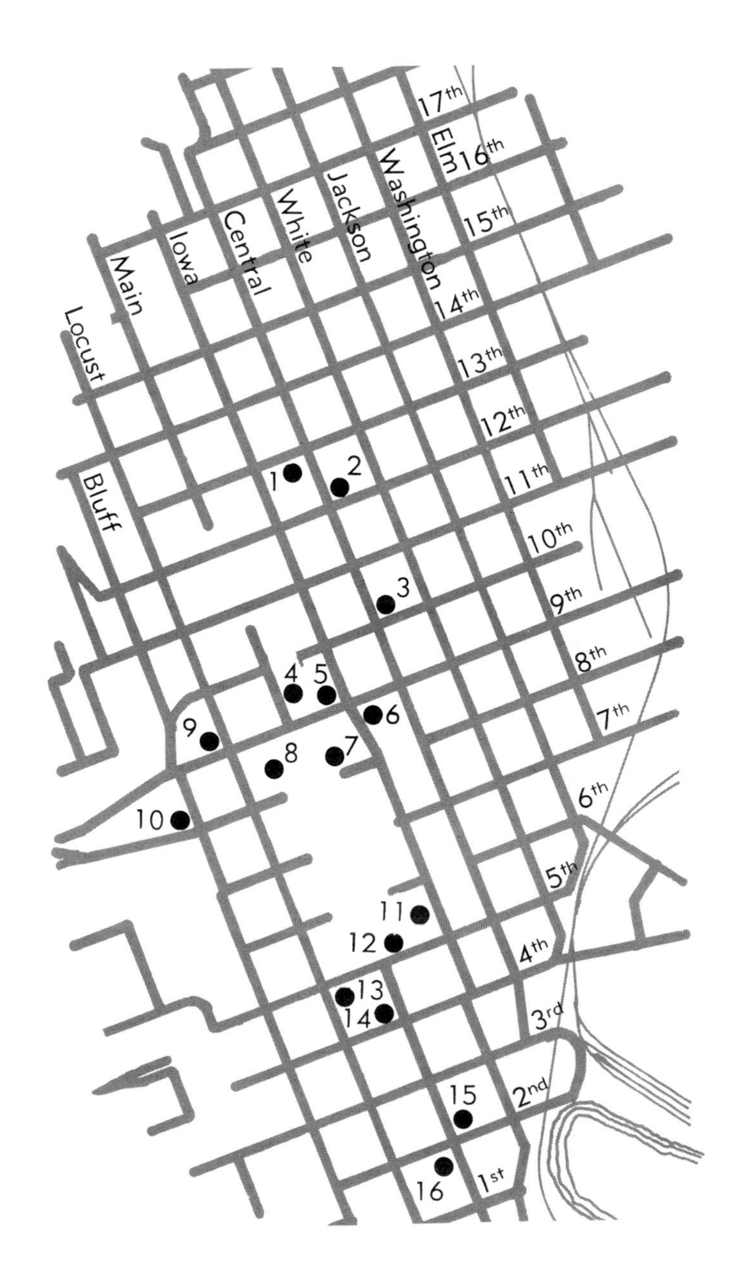

ter itself was a cubical box with the stage opening from one side.

The backdrop filled the proscenium opening and most of the action took place on the wide stage apron that projected into the auditorium. On either side of the stage were two or more levels of box seats, while the remaining seating was divided between the main floor and two shallow galleries along the rear and side walls.

By the 1870's a new quest for realism changed the theatrical world. The action moved within the proscenium where the setting could completely surround the performers. The creation of the so-called "box set" precipitated a revolution in theater design. Because the ideal viewpoint for such a setting is directly in front of the stage, the formerly-glamorous box seats became the worst seats in the house. In Dubuque's Orpheum the nineteenth-century stage apron has disappeared, and the main floor has forward-facing seats. On either side, however, the old box seats and shallow "dress circle" gallery remains. Above this level is a deep balcony that looks directly down on the stage, a forerunner of the large balconies that would be found in the theaters of the 1920's. One other vestige of nineteenth-century design can also be seen in the Orpheum. It is the third level balcony, the old Family Circle, complete with its separate entry and high backed benches, features that would have been familiar to audiences of the Civil War era.

The restored Orpheum has become one of Downtown Dubuque's most impressive structures. Dubuque is fortunate that the building even stands. Almost lost to the wrecking ball of the downtown urban renewal project, it was only at the eleventh hour that a handful of concerned local citizens were able to save the theater by proposing to convert it to a community auditorium that would serve as the focal point of a proposed Five Flags Civic Center. When work is completed the Baroque-like interior of the auditorium will seat nearly 1,000 people during concerts, plays and a variety of other activities. The exterior restoration dramatically displays the original appearance of this important landmark and represents some of the finest such historic preservation activity that has been undertaken in Dubuque. Because of both its historical and architectural significance, the Orpheum is listed on the National Register of Historic Places.

The Grand Opera House at Eighth and Iowa is another important Dubuque theater that has survived to the present. Now a motion picture house, the building's history dates back to the late 1880's.

As early as 1882, only six years after the opening of the Duncan-Waller Opera House, the local press reported that a movement was underway to erect a new opera house. The Grand Opera House Corporation was formed, and a successful public subscription campaign was launched.

Construction began in 1889, and the Grand opened in August, 1890. Gas fixtures were installed until a dynamo could be connected to generate electric power

Grand Opera House

for the theater. The Grand's seating capacity was 848. Its stage house was substantially larger than any previous Dubuque theater. The proscenium opening was thirty-five feet wide and twenty-five feet high, and the total stage depth was forty-two feet. The rigging loft was seventy feet high and contained sixty sets of lines.

For the first thirty years of its existence, the Grand Opera House attracted Dubuque's "carriage trade" to the best of legitimate theater. Complete financial records for the Grand exist to 1932. The figures demonstrate the phenomenal rise in receipts from "moving pictures" compared to the declining receipts of legitimate theater. Thus, today, the Grand stands as a theater of transition: from the best of the legitimate stage era to the heyday of motion picture entertainment.[11]

At the same time that Dubuque's Orpheum Theater was being built a Neo-Classical Revivalist movement was affecting American architecture. This was a peculiarly American development that had no parallel abroad. The Columbian Exposition of 1893 at Chicago and the Pan American Exhibition of 1901 at Buffalo played major roles in the movement to recreate classical buildings of monumental scale. The Fine Arts Building at the 1893 Exposition foreshadowed the movement while McKim, Mead and White's Pennsylvania Station in New York City was its major monument. Nearly all the examples were public buildings. The extent of the Neo-Classical Revival movement's impact can be measured by the facts that it affected most American cities,

Carnegie Stout Library

First Church of Christ Scientist

and that between 1900 and 1917 more marble was used in the United States than was used in the Roman Empire during its entire history.[12]

At least three Dubuque buildings exhibit features of Neo-Classical Revival architecture. The Carnegie-Stout Public Library at Eleventh and Bluff illustrates a Grecian version complete with monumentally-scaled Corinthian columns supporting the traditional pedimented portico. Matching pilasters can be seen behind each column. The notched dentils along the cornice and gable of the pediment are other classical Greek elements. The library was built in 1901 with the aid of an Andrew Carnegie grant on land donated by F. D. Stout. The building itself cost $60,000.

Another interpretation of the Neo-Classical Style can be seen in the First Church of Christ Scientist at Ninth and Bluff. Here Roman elements dominate as illustrated by the simplified columns and ornament. The classical proportions of the temple can be seen in the gable of the facade. The church cost $40,000 when it was built in 1911.

One other revivalist movement flourished during the first quarter of the twentieth century and is represented by several Dubuque houses.

> The Georgian house on its high foundation with its imposing entrance and well balanced exterior was the embodiment of genteel formality. The principal features of such a house were the wide paneled door . . . There might be a window at one or both sides of the door and above it there would usually be a fanlight . . .

> The roof could be low-gabled to permit a well-proportioned classical pediment, or be a gambrel or even hipped. A classical cornice could replace the traditional eaves. Dormers, if any, would be narrow with a triangular pediment. Sometimes the roof ridge would be flattened to form a deck or "widow's walk." The Georgian chimney would usually be plain.[13]

690 Fenelon Place

The development of Georgian Revival design in Dubuque can be traced back to the Civil War. Two houses on Fenelon Place illustrate early Georgian Revival characteristics. The Cunningham house at 690 Fenelon was built in 1865 and is one of the earliest homes in the area. Nearby at 710 Fenelon is another Georgian house of the same era. This well-maintained house was built by the Cox family. It exhibits many traditional characteristics that would later be incorporated into the numerous Georgian Revival designs that were built between about 1900 and 1920.

888 Yale Court

Another early Dubuque example of Georgian architecture can be seen at 888 Yale Court. The old Herancourt family house was built by a furniture maker who came to Dubuque from Bavaria in 1845. He finished the house himself using finely-worked pine for all the woodwork including the ten fireplaces. Basically similar to many other Dubuque houses of the period, the Herancourt house reflects the very beginnings of the Georgian Revival movement as evidenced by the doorway, chimneys and rooftop deck.

In contrast to these early examples, twentieth-century Georgian Revival architecture in Dubuque exhibits

710 Fenelon Place

1090 Langworthy Avenue

1595 Montrose Terrace

varied interpretations of the style, even incorporating detailed elements from other styles as well. The late Georgian Revival house might have a classical portico of immense proportions as illustrated by two Dubuque houses at 1595 Montrose and 1090 Langworthy. The house on Montrose possesses what must surely be the most overwhelming portico in the city. There are actually two porches. One provides a full length deck for the second floor and is supported by four columns. Protruding above this large-enough porch is a massive third story porch supported by two very large columns. The decks of both porches provide excellent vantage points for viewing the town and river.

In contrast to the Roman character of the portico of the house on Montrose, the house on Langworthy Street exhibits a two-story Greek portico. The fluted columns contrast with the plain Roman columns of the other house and support a classically-proportioned triangular pediment. Built by Joseph Garland, a Dubuque businessman, the facade of this house exhibits many of the characteristic Georgian Revival features including the fanlit door, overall symmetry and small dormers. Other features of interest include an unusual side entrance, a small swimming pool in the basement and a unique ventilation system utilizing an underground tunnel for a cool air supply.

Other local variations of the Georgian Revival style can be seen in houses at 340 Wartburg Place, 2441 Broadway and 389 Hill Street.

2441 Broadway Street

340 Wartburg Place

389 Hill Street

Between the outbreak of World War I and the Great Depression that followed the stock market crash of 1929, the development of Dubuque's architectural heritage manifested itself in several ways. By this time rising costs, a shortage of skilled craftsmen, along with a lack of interest on the part of most people, curtailed construction of buildings in most of the revivalist styles common in Dubuque prior to the turn of the century. In their place varied "modern" styles appeared. Excellent local examples of Bungaloid, Prairie Style, International, Modernistic and Spanish Colonial Revival styles can be seen by driving around those portions of Dubuque that were built up after World War I. Once again, architectural pattern books and magazines furnished the ideas and promoted the construction of "modern" houses in many of the latest styles.

One unique Dubuque house illustrates how architectural styles developed during the 1920's. Dubuque's first all electric house was constructed in 1924 by John G. Kuehnle, owner of the Dubuque Electric Company. It is located at Kirkwood and Alta Vista and was described as a model home incorporating all of the very latest innovations in electrical living. Even today the idea of using waste heat from the house to heat the garage would be considered novel. Local firms donated most of the materials used. Described in a newspaper as being in the "English Style," the house is actually an example of Bungaloid architecture, one of the more "Americanized" architectural developments of the early twentieth century.

Kirkwood and Alta Vista Streets

Based on early nineteenth-century British models found in India, the Bungaloid Style flourished first in California between 1900 and 1920. California bungalows became so common that standardized sets of plans could be purchased for as little as $5.00. There were numerous variations on the bungaloid theme, but all took their character from their small size, simplicity and economical construction. The true bungalow was of one story but many houses that had two stories were made to look like bungalows. The houses at 95 South Grandview, 125 South Grandview, and 1781 Plymouth all typify the traditional bungaloid architectural concepts and demonstrate the idea that:

> It was the bungalow as much as any other kind of house that led to the general adoption of the "living room" and the "outdoor-indoor" living space—of craftsmanship, climatic adaptation and harmony with the landscape.[14]

1781 Plymouth Street

125 South Grandview Avenue

95 South Grandview Avenue

999 Kirkwood Street

1105 Highland Place

Two houses in the Spanish Colonial Revival Style are located at 1105 Highland and 999 Kirkwood. Typical features of this southwestern United States inspired style are low-pitched tile roofs or flat roofs surrounded by parapets, arches, plastered walls and carved or cast ornament. Balconies of wrought iron and window grills are also common. Such houses take many forms as the two Dubuque examples illustrate. Although the Kirkwood Street house is built of brick, both are good examples of this western style adapted to the Midwest.

The so-called International Style is characterized by complete absence of ornament and by shapes in which the effects of mass and weight are minimized for the sake of an effect of pure volume.[15] Flat roofs, smooth uniform wall surfaces and windows that are perceived as continuations of the walls are other key features. Walls are normally plastered or painted white. Based upon principles developed by Walter Gropius, Mies van der Rohe and Le Corbusier in Europe during the 1920's, the International Style was the predominant modern architecture of the 1930's. By World War II the style was being criticized because of its severity, but it has been said that no architect since could design as if the International Style had never existed.[16]

Among others, Dubuque has three excellent examples of International Style houses at 120, 155 and 1144 South Grandview.

155 South Grandview Avenue

1144 South Grandview Avenue

120 South Grandview Avenue

Although Frank Lloyd Wright never designed any buildings in Dubuque, his influence was nevertheless felt by the builders of at least two local structures. The general characteristics of Prairie Style architecture can be seen in the house at 1761 Plymouth Street, and the Eagle Point Park Pavilion illustrates many aspects of Wrightian design.

The basis for many of Wright's concepts came from his contacts with both the Midwestern prairie environment and from Japan. He wrote:

> We of the Middle West are living on the prairie. The prairie has a beauty of its own and we should recognize and accentuate this natural beauty, its quiet level. Hence gently sloping roofs, low proportions, quiet sky lines, suppressed heavy-set chimneys and sheltering overhangs, low terraces and out-reaching walls sequestering private gardens.[17]

Accordingly, Prairie Style architecture emphasizes horizontal planes. Roofs are low with wide projecting eaves. Most such houses are of two stories but often have single story wings reaching out in different directions. Ribbon windows with wood casements carry on the horizontal theme. Plaster over a wood frame is the most common type of construction, but brick and even stone may be used. Wright was the acknowledged master of Prairie Style design, but he had many imitators, most of whom were architects whose only contact with Wright was through the drawings found in architectural magazines.

In contrast to the straightforward interpretation of Prairie Style design of the house on Plymouth Street,

1761 Plymouth Street

the Eagle Point Park Pavilion illustrates another aspect of Wright's influence on American architecture. The use of native materials is well illustrated by this somewhat unusual structure that appears to actually grow out of the rock from which it is built.

The pavilion along with the beautiful rock gardens and several other Eagle Point Park buildings were designed and built by Dubuque Park Superintendent Alfred Caldwell during the Great Depression of the 1930's. Caldwell was hired by the City of Dubuque to carry out the WPA sponsored park development. A gifted landscape architect with training and experience in engineering, architecture, stone cutting and masonry as well as forestry, botany and plant ecology, Caldwell both designed and built the Eagle Point Park buildings and gardens. He was just thirty-one years old when the city hired him at an annual salary of less than $2,000, but his experience included work for the Chicago Park Board and three years of association with Jens Jensen, a Chicago landscape architect of international reputation. It is interesting to note that Caldwell's application for the Dubuque position included a letter of recommendation from Jensen that described him as "a genius and the outstanding prospect as a landscape gardener in this country."[18] Caldwell's genius manifested itself in his work at Eagle Point Park. Of his structures there, he said:

> In a small park much might be done. It is out of the nature of things that the cheapest and nearest to hand, properly understood, is the best and most beautiful. All ugliness is expensive and certainly expensive to build.[19]

Caldwell's exceptional use of native construction materials, craftsmanship and unique designs make his Eagle Point Park pavilion among the most significant buildings in Dubuque. In addition, his overall impact on the development of the park has made it one of the most beautiful in Iowa.

The frantic activity of the 1920's followed by the Great Depression of the 1930's brought change to the architectural profession. Architecture became a genteel profession . . .

> suitable for the man who had attended an Ivy League college, made the Grand Tour of Europe, caught the lively spirit of the *Ecole des Beaux Arts,* knew his wines and brandies and old chateux, married a suitably wealthy and cultivated wife and could stage grandiose settings for wealthier men whom he knew at social clubs.[20]

In Dubuque, the changing trends of the twenties were reflected in a number of ways. Building began to slow even before the Great Depression struck. With the coming of the Depression, however, the city entered upon a period of economic and population stability that lasted until after World War II. This long period of *status quo* is undoubtedly a major reason why so much of Dubuque's nineteenth-century architectural heritage has remained. There were simply no pressures for demolishing many old buildings, but neglect and decay did take their toll. From 1900 until 1930 the number of local architects showed a gradual decline.

Compared to the florid and varied designs of the nineteenth century, the level of local domestic architecture was quite modest. In fact, even the anonymous vernacular houses of the 1870's and 1880's are more noticeable than the typical houses of the 1920's and 1930's that fill the subdivisions of these later years. Some important stylistic developments of the early twentieth century do not appear in Dubuque at all. The late Gothic Revival and Jacobethan Revival designs so characteristic of much post-1900 religious and collegiate architecture did not fully develop in Dubuque. The geometrical ornament and vertical mass of Modernistic or Art Deco Style commercial building, however, can be found in the present Dubuque post office and federal building. Built in 1934

Dubuque Post Office

of Indiana limestone, the post office is the best local example of Modernistic design but art deco details can also be found on the Masonic Temple on Locust Street and the old Medical Associates building on Main Street.

With the exception of a very few recent landmarks and the development of the western subdivisions filled with the domestic designs of the mid-twentieth century, the unique architectural character of Dubuque was firmly established by the time the stock market crashed in 1929. Dubuque's architectural heritage can best be found in the hundreds of local buildings that date from the Victorian decades of the nineteenth century. In comparison, the post-1900 period produced only a few moments of architectural diversion. This should not be considered unfortunate, however, for many Midwestern cities are built on the architectural foundations of the twentieth century, while few possess the richness of nineteenth-century design found in Dubuque.

Preserving The Heritage of Dubuque

Preserving The Heritage of Dubuque

Much has been written about Dubuque's history, its scenic beauty, and its unique character. Yet until recently, most historic preservation activities in Dubuque, as in many other places, have been undertaken in a random manner, usually in response to a crisis and for the sake of a few major landmarks. The majority of Dubuque's vast collection of historical and architecturally significant landmarks has generally been ignored.

Obviously, not every old structure in a place like Dubuque can or should be saved. Many probably should not be. But at the same time, no building should be torn down merely because it is old. Those structures that contribute significantly to the city's heritage should be preserved as well as others of architectural interest that contribute to Dubuque's urban character. With few exceptions, economically feasible modern uses can be found for old buildings of almost any kind – if imagination and an earnest desire to save them exist.

Any type of historic preservation activity, if it is to be successful, must consider more than outstanding landmarks. Very few of Dubuque's old buildings are of national importance, but many do have significance from a regional and local point of view. It is these lesser buildings that shape much of Dubuque's unique character and provide the key for creative preservation efforts.

Dubuque's old buildings can teach us much about the city's past growth, economic conditions, social values and way of life. In addition, the city's historical and architecturally significant structures can teach us much about the present. By retaining buildings and other structures from earlier periods of Dubuque history, we are in a better position to judge our contemporary values and progress toward a higher quality of life. Because we presently live in an era of unbelievably rapid change, with new technologies altering our lives on almost a daily basis, it is increasingly difficult to put one's personal existence in perspective. All people, and particularly people who live in cities, need ways to recognize and hold their cultural and physical roots. In places like Dubuque, the city's unique natural and man-made features can satisfy at least part of this need by serving as visible reminders of the past. As a minimum, the best from every age of the city's development should be saved. Ways must also be found to resolve present conflicts between preservation and change so that the best of the new can be successfully integrated with the best of the old. Throughout the United States, the continued loss of old buildings has given surviving ones added significance. In Dubuque itself, the county jail, shot tower and Fenelon Place Elevator are only three examples of historical or architecturally significant structures that have national importance because of their rarity.

In general, the values of old buildings are many. Some may be the location of historic events. Some may be associated with notable persons. Some may possess distinctive architectural and artistic features while others may simply be interesting as curiosities. In every case, however, they contribute to the variety and vitality of the urban scene.

Traditionally, there have been a variety of approaches to solving preservation problems. Often both public and private resources are joined to achieve outstanding results. Locally, the Newman log cabin, Mathias Ham house, Shot Tower and Orpheum Theater all owe their preservation to joint public-private efforts that, in some instances, date back to the early decades of the twentieth century. On the other hand, literally dozens of Dubuque's most interesting old houses have been preserved solely as the result of individual concern and care. Within the last few years these old houses, often in dilapidated condition, have taken on new value for purchase and rehabilitation by imaginative persons.

Dubuque's old world charm and character is largely the result of its river bluff setting and its nineteenth-century architecture. From every bluff varied house types can be seen. They range from simple cottages to elaborate mansions. The many churches reflect a strong religious heritage and also contribute greatly to the city's urban appearance.

Historic preservation activities in Dubuque must obviously be concerned with the great nineteenth-

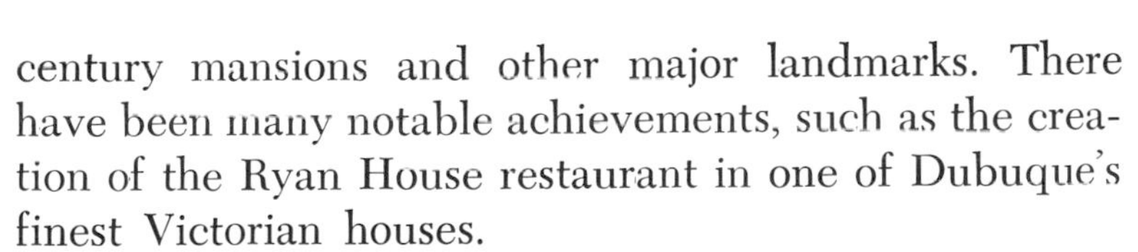

century mansions and other major landmarks. There have been many notable achievements, such as the creation of the Ryan House restaurant in one of Dubuque's finest Victorian houses.

Downtown Dubuque has been the scene of some major preservation accomplishments. The town clock has been moved to a new location and is now the focal point of Town Clock Plaza. The largest preservation project ever undertaken in Dubuque has been the adaptation of the old Roshek department store into the most modern office block in the city. But perhaps the most striking achievement has been the restoration of the Orpheum Theater. It is once again one of the most handsome buildings on Main Street. The Dubuque County Court House is also undergoing exterior restoration as part of a long-range modernization program. Hopefully, the unique Egyptian Revival jail can also be saved.

Local preservation activity, however, has not been limited to major landmarks. Throughout Dubuque old houses of every description have been carefully restored and modernized without destroying their architectural character.

One imaginative local project, sponsored by private interests, has been the development of Cable Car Square, an area of small shops near the base of the Fenelon Place Elevator. Several old and deteriorating buildings have been renovated to include shops and offices on lower floors with apartments above.

Local preservationists are becoming more concerned about entire neighborhoods and street frontages as well as individual structures. Recently, the Dubuque City Council adopted a demolition review ordinance aimed specifically at strengthening preservation potential within designated areas of architectural importance. A new zoning ordinance will also provide additional preservation opportunities.

One particularly interesting aspect of Dubuque's architectural heritage is the great variety of structural detail found on buildings of all types. A bit of carving above a window, the solid turret at the corner of a mansion, an old cast iron street lamp and even the delicate scroll of a sign bracket over an entry all help give Dubuque its special richness.

Whatever the purpose or scope of any local preservation program, however, the goal should remain the same, namely to assure that the buildings and areas that make Dubuque unique are maintained in such a way that they contribute actively to our modern society either in their original role or in a suitable new one. Cities of every size need a mingling of old buildings mixed with the new. Innovative historic preservation programs can help provide such urban diversity.

Orpheum Theater (page 129)

Glossary of Architectural Terms

Balloon Frame
A house frame built up from small dimension timbers, usually two by fours, nailed together.

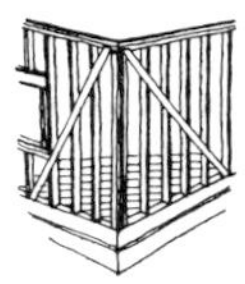

Bargeboard
A board, often decorative, covering the projecting rafter of the gable end of a roof. Also called a vergeboard.

Belvedere
A structure affording an extensive view usually located on the roof top of a dwelling, but sometimes an independent building.

Bracket
A small projection, usually decorated, that supports or appears to support an overhanging cornice, gable or sill.

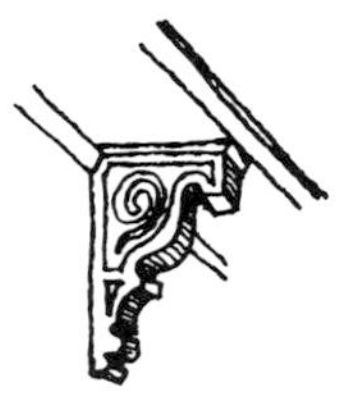

Buttress
A mass of masonry built at right angles to one of the main outer walls of a building to help it resist lateral forces. Buttresses are common on churches that have vaulted or arched ceilings.

Clapboard
Narrow, horizontal, overlapping wooden boards, usually four to six inches wide, used as siding.

Corbel
A projection from a masonry wall or other feature sometimes used to support a load and sometimes merely for decoration.

Cornice
A molding at the edge of a roof. Also any continuous molded and projecting cap to a wall or window.

Cresting
Light, repeated ornament that is incised or perforated and carried along the top of a wall or roof.

Cupola
A small, domed structure rising from a roof or tower.

Dentil
One of a series of small rectangular blocks similar in effect to teeth and often found in the lower part of a cornice.

Dormer
A structure built into a sloping roof.

Fanlight
An overdoor window, usually semi-elliptical or semi-circular in shape.

Facade
The face or elevation of a building.

Gable
The above eave portion of the end wall of a building having a pitched or gambrel roof. The term is sometimes used to refer to the entire end wall.

Gambrel Roof
A ridged roof with the slope broken on each side.

Gingerbread
Pierced curvilinear ornament executed with a jig saw or scroll saw and placed under the eaves.

Hipped Roof
A roof with slopes on all four sides.

Hood
A dripstone or projecting molding over the head of doorways, windows or arches to throw off rain.

Imbrication
An overlapping after the manner of scales of a pine cone. Usually refers to a pattern of shingling.

Lintel
A horizontal member that supports the load over the opening of a door or window.

Mansard Roof
In effect, a hipped gambrel roof. It has two slopes, the lower being steeper than the upper.

Orders
In classical architecture an order consists of a column, its capital or head and the horizontal entablature above which it supports. These were proportioned and decorated according to certain modes. The Doric, Ionic and Corinthian modes of the Greeks were later modified by the Romans who added three more of their own, the Tuscan, Roman Doric and Composite, the latter being a synthesis of the Greek Ionic and Corinthian orders.

Palladian Window
A Renaissance style window consisting of treating three openings as one, the center one arched and wider.

Pediment
The gable end of a roof or a feature resembling it. Usually refers to classical architecture.

Pilaster
A feature in the shape of a pillar but only projecting slightly from the wall. Pilasters are designed to simulate a column with a capital.

Pointing
The outer and visible finish of the mortar between the bricks or stones of a masonry wall.

Portico
A large porch having a roof, often with a pediment and supported by columns or pillars.

Quoin
An outside corner of a building or one of the stones or bricks forming an outside corner.

Rose Window
A circular window whose mullions converge like the spokes of a wheel. Also called a wheel window.

Row House
A house joined to its neighbor by a party wall and covered by a common roof.

Rubble Stone
Stones that have not been shaped or at most shaped by fracture. In walls of coursed rubble the stones are approximately the same size and the courses clearly defined. In walls of random rubble the stones are of varying size and shape and the pattern formed is quite irregular.

Terra Cotta
Earth baked or burnt in molds for use in building construction and decoration, harder in quality than brick.

Tracery
Ornamental openwork of stone in the upper part of a Gothic window. In Gothic Revival buildings the tracery is often of wood or iron.

Turret
A small tower, often hung on the corner of a building.

Veranda
A space alongside a house sheltered by a roof supported by posts.

Dubuque Architects Listed In City Directories 1857-1929

The following list summarizes the practicing architects in Dubuque for select years between 1857 and 1929. The list is based on information available in city directories.

Particularly during the early years, many of the persons listed as architects were contractors or builders as well. Until the establishment of a trained architectural profession relatively late in the nineteenth century it was common practice for an "architect" to also be a builder. With few exceptions it was not possible until after the Civil War for an architect to make a living solely by designing buildings for others to construct.

One should note that the commercial listings in the city directories commonly had to be paid for as advertising. Thus, the listings for architects, builders and other craftsmen may not be one-hundred percent complete. In any given year some persons undoubtedly chose not to purchase a listing. This fact would partially explain some of the variations in listings for different years. At the same time, however, at least some measure of the relative economic and building activity in Dubuque can be ascertained from the numbers of architects, contractors, brickmakers, stonemasons and other craftsmen listed in the directories.

1857 Dubuque City Directory

Name	Address
J. D. Abry	Washington between 10th and 11th
W. S. Allardyce	111 Main
William Baumer	White between 11th and 12th
S. Y. Bradstreet	Nevada between Julien and 5th
F. G. Brandt	17 Rebman's Block
A. Harris	63 Main
William Longhurst	11 Shine's Block
J. M. Moody	12 Rebman's Block
John Mullany	Bluff between 7th and 8th
G. W. Osborn	Washington between 19th and 20th
Rague and Drake	124 Main
L. L. Wood	Bluff between 9th and 10th

1860 Dubuque City Directory

J. D. Abry	15th between Clay and White
W. S. Allardyce	10th and Jackson
A. G. Bale	4th between Locust and Bluff
F. G. Brandt	126 Main
A. C. Diboll	Bluff between 7th and 8th
W. E. Greathead	Locust and 13th
I. Hanson	Rose and Race
Jones and Son	15th and Iowa
S. Logan	Iowa between 9th and 10th
Wm. Longhurst	Race between 11th and Rose
W. Metcalf	4th between Locust and Bluff
Owens and Bros.	Main and 11th
J. G. Peterson	13th between Main and Iowa
J. F. Rague	Seminary Bluff

1870 Dubuque City Directory

C. H. Henderson and F. G. Brandt	9th between Main and Iowa
J. Keenan	3rd and Bluff
J. Mullany	5th between Main and Locust

1880 Dubuque City Directory

R. Armstrong	Julien Avenue near Hill
J. Bell	Locust between 9th and 10th
G. R. Clark	10th between Main and Iowa
C. G. Esson	8th between Locust and Bluff
M. Flick	Iowa between 16th and 17th
F. Heer	299 7th
O. Holland	Julien near Bluff
J. Howie	255 5th
F. D. Hyde	7th and Main
J. Keenan	W. 3rd near Bluff
J. McCoy	240 9th
Oeth and Trexler	1690 Jackson
L. B. Tuttle	5th and Iowa
C. A. Wilber	Grove Terrace near W. 11th

1890 Dubuque City Directory

Beck & Heer	13th and Clay
Wm. Gill	120 2nd
F. Heer & Son	327 8th
F. D. Hyde	7th and Main
J. Keenan	W. 3rd
C. A. Wilbur	7 Grove Terrace

1900 Dubuque City Directory

G. Beck	805 Main
T. T. Carkeek	Lincoln Block
G. F. Guilbert	Bank and Insurance Building
F. Heer & Son	325 8th
M. Heer	1301 Clay
J. Keenan	31 W. 3rd
J. Spencer	Bank & Insurance Building
C. A. Wilbur	7 Grove Terrace

1909 Dubuque City Directory

G. Beck	815 Main
C. Bush	38 8th
T. T. Carkeek	121 8th
F. Heer & Son	325 8th
M. Heer	1301 Clay
J. Spencer	Bank & Insurance Building

1921 Dubuque City Directory

T. T. Carkeek	17 Lincoln Building
F. Heer & Son	Bank & Insurance Building
J. F. Leith	422 Main
K. F. Saam	410 Main

1929 Dubuque City Directory

N. W. Fisher	1107 Federal Bank Building
F. Heer & Son	Bank & Insurance Building
C. I. Krajewski	730 Main
K. F. Saam	730 Main

Some Designs of Prominent Dubuque Architects

John F. Rague

Rague was born in New Jersey in 1799. He received his architectural training at the New York office of Minard Lafever. After living in New York for several years he moved to Springfield, Illinois where he lived until 1844. While in Springfield, he supervised the construction of the Illinois capitol and designed the first capitol of Iowa at Iowa City. From 1844 until he moved to Dubuque in 1854 Rague lived in Milwaukee and designed several buildings at Milwaukee, Chicago, Madison and Janesville. Between 1855 and 1860 Rague designed some of Dubuque's most important landmarks. His local works included:

Dubuque City Hall
13th and Central

Dubuque County Jail
8th and Central

F. E. Bissell House
11th between Bluff and Locust

Addition to Old Dubuque County Court House
7th and Central

Goodrich-Wilson-Ryan House
1243 Locust Street

Edward Langworthy House
1095 W. Third Street

First Ward (Franklin) School
Bluff and Jones

Third Ward (Prescott) School
12th & Clay

Fifth Ward (Audubon) School
Johnson & Lincoln

Fridolin J. Heer & Son

The son of a master builder, Fridolin J. Heer was born at Wallenstadt, Canton St. Gallen, Switzerland in 1834. For six years he was apprenticed to a master stonecutter at Rapperswill. After his apprenticeship, Heer traveled through northern Germany before spending two years studying art in Munich. In 1860 he established himself as a master stonecutter in Chur, Canton Granbrundten and erected many important monuments in area towns during the next five years. After the death of a friend created financial problems in 1865, Heer left Switzerland for Chicago. He worked in Chicago and Bellevue, Illinois before moving to Dubuque in 1868. From 1868 until 1870 Heer worked as a stonecutter. In 1870 he opened an architectural practice and became one of Dubuque's leading architects until his death in 1910. Fridolin Heer Jr., his son, joined the firm in 1887 after studying at the School of Architecture at Stuttgart, Germany. After the elder Heer's death, his son continued the architectural practice until 1934. The firm's many designs included some of the most important landmarks ever constructed in Dubuque. A partial listing follows:

James Levi Store, 1871
7th and Main

Globe Building
5th and Main

Michel Building
Main near 5th

Town Clock Building, 1873
Main between 8th and 9th

Eagle Building
9th and Main

W. J. Knight House
1397 Main

William Bradley House
1268 Locust

Col. Wm. Henderson House
1433 Main

A. J. Van Duzee House
1471 Main

Alex. Young House, 1879
(Behr Funeral Home)
1491 Main

William Andrew House
1135 Locust

A. Tredway House
1182 Locust

Mt. St. Joseph Academy Building
Clarke College Campus

Additions to Motherhouse
for Sisters of St. Francis
Davis Street

Additions to St. Mary's
Orphanage, 1882
Sheridan Road

Irving School
Delhi Street

Fischer Ice & Cold Storage
East 4th Street Extension

Office Block
3rd & Iowa

First Security Building, 1901-02
8th and Main

Jaeger Hardware Building, 1901
768 Main

M. M. Hoffmann Funeral Home, 1890
15th & Clay

Additions to Mary of the Angels
Home, 6th & Bluff

H. L. Stout House
1145 Locust

L. Gonner House
1295 Alta Vista

N. J. Schrup House
14th and Main

W. S. Molo House
16th and Locust

F. A. Rumpf House
W. 11th Street

Alphonse Matthews House
1335 Locust

A. F. Heeb House
15 Jefferson

Telegraph Herald Building
7th and Main

Dubuque County Court House, 1891
7th and Central

Sacred Heart Church & School, 1887
W. 22nd Street

Sunnycrest Sanatorium, 1919-21
Roosevelt Avenue

St. Joseph Academy, 1894
13th & Main

Fulton School
Central between 22nd & 23rd

Jackson School
West Locust

Brunswick-Balke-Collender
Buildings
Dubuque

Additions to Julien House
2nd & Main

St. Columbkille's School
Rush Street

J. Frantzen Residence

J. Schwind Residence

J. T. Hancock Residence
11 Highland Place

Thomas T. Carkeek

Thomas Carkeek was born in 1843 at Redruth, Cornwall in the southwest of England. He followed his father's trade of stonemason and also learned carpentry before immigrating to Wisconsin. By 1882 he had moved to Dubuque and was employed by Carr, Ryder & Wheeler Company as an architect. Ten years later he opened his own practice in the Lincoln building. Between 1891 and 1911 Carkeek is said to have designed over 200 Dubuque buildings. A few of his designs included:

Lincoln Building
8th and Locust

Central Engine House
9th and Iowa

Odd Fellows Building
9th and Locust

Rider, Burden & Rider Building
7th and Locust

Bell Bros. Building
4th and Locust

John Ernsdorff Sons Co.
Main and Jones

Norwegian Plow Co. Building
Jones and S. Main

M. M. Walker Building
Jones & Main

Schroeder & Kleine Building
90 S. Main

"Redstone", A. A. Cooper House
504 Bluff

C. H. Gregories House
109 Alpine

Fred. Bell House
968 W. 3rd.

D. J. Lenehan House
41 Cornell

G. W. Healey House
701 Bluff

Jas. Forrestor's Building
4th and Iowa

Bradley and Sullivan Building
Main, between 6th and 7th

B. W. Lacy Building
15th & Clay

Hotel Paris
4th and Clay

Elberon Flats
11th and Iowa

Arno Flats
11th and Iowa

Florence Flats
13th & Main

G. A. Burden Flats

I. J. Cushing House
2 mi. N.E. of Dubuque

I. Harris House
349 Hill

I. Cleminson House
575 W. Third

W. H. Day Jr. House
66 Highland Place

C. Mathis House
118 Broadway

J. Lenihan Double House
5th and Hill

East Dubuque Public School
East Dubuque, Illinois

East Dubuque Engine House
East Dubuque, Illinois

Some Dubuque Building Craftsmen

Local historical records contain much information about the city's prominent residents, and we also know a great deal about the landmark structures of Dubuque. In contrast, very little is known about the individual craftsmen who actually worked on many of the buildings that are considered historical or architecturally significant today.

The following list of building craftsmen represents an attempt to shed some light on the high level of construction craftsmanship that was achieved during the late nineteenth and early twentieth centuries. By identifying the ethnic and cultural background of at least a few of the many carpenters, brickmasons, stonecutters and other craftsmen who worked in Dubuque it may be possible to better understand the city's present architectural character.

CARPENTERS AND BUILDERS

John Bell

Born in Scotland in 1827, Bell immigrated to Montreal in 1844 where he lived until moving to Dubuque in 1853. Upon his arrival in the Key City, he established himself as a carpenter and worked on many local buildings for the next thirty years.

B. W. Jones

Jones was born in 1837 at Manchester, England. He came to the U.S. in 1845 and settled at Dubuque in 1856. Until late in the century he engaged in contract building and also served as an alderman in 1879.

John Keenan

An Irishman by birth, Keenan arrived in Philadelphia in 1842 at age eighteen. From 1854 until well into the 1880's he was a local carpenter and builder.

John McCoy

McCoy was born in Cork, Ireland and immigrated to America in 1850. He learned carpentry in Rochester, New York before moving to Dubuque in 1856. During the 1860's and 1870's McCoy worked on many local buildings.

N. P. Nicks

A native Dubuquer, born in 1848, Nicks learned the carpentry trade while working for others before establishing his own building firm in 1882.

William Rebman

A native of Pennsylvania, Rebman came to Dubuque in 1837. From 1837 to 1850 he worked as a blacksmith before turning to real estate and contracting. He constructed many downtown buildings and was also responsible for much local street work as well as the grading of Washington Park.

John Trexler

Trexler learned carpentry and woodcarving in his native Bavaria where he was born in 1825. He came to America in 1852 and settled at Dubuque in 1855 where he worked as a carpenter until his death.

L. B. Tuttle

Tuttle was born in Connecticut. He moved to Dubuque in 1858 where he learned the carpentry trade and worked for many years as a local builder.

BRICKMAKERS

John Dietrich

Dietrich was born in Prussia in 1827. From 1855 until 1874 he worked as a plasterer and lime maker in Dubuque. From 1874 until his death he operated his own brickyard and made 700,000 to 1,000,000 bricks annually.

Diedrich Muggenburg

Born in Germany in 1923, Muggenburg came to the U.S. in 1854. He settled at Dubuque in 1855 where he worked in a brickyard until 1876. In that year he opened his own operation that produced 700,000 bricks per year.

Bernard J. O'Neill

O'Neill was born in Ireland in 1846 and came to Dubuque in 1852. He engaged in the grain business but also made and sold over 10,000,000 bricks between 1870 and 1880.

August Roeber

A native of Germany, Roeber immigrated to the U.S. in 1860 and arrived at Dubuque in 1870. His brickyard was located near Eagle Point and manufactured over 1,000,000 bricks per year.

STONECUTTERS AND MASONS

Alois Fricke

Alois Fricke, born in Switzerland in 1818, came to Galena in 1845 and then to Dubuque a year later. He worked as a brick and stonemason until the early 1880's building many local buildings that included the Lorimier House hotel at Bluff and Eighth and the Mt. St. Joseph Academy buildings on what is now the Clarke College campus.

August Jungk

Born in 1818 in Saxony, August Jungk emigrated in 1837 and finally settled at Dubuque in 1850. For the following thirty years he worked as a local stonecutter.

John P. Meyers

A Prussian by birth, Meyers had already learned stonecutting before coming to the U.S. at age nineteen in 1853. He worked at his trade in Dubuque from 1855 until his death.

Peter Mihm

Mihm was born in 1827. He learned stonecutting in his native Bavaria before moving to Pennsylvania in 1852. He arrived at Dubuque in 1855 and worked on many Dubuque buildings for the next thirty years.

Andrew Pfiffner

Pfiffner was only fifteen years old when he immigrated to Dubuque from his native Switzerland. Both Andrew and his brother, Martin, cut stone for several Dubuque buildings.

M. H. Schilling

A bricklayer, Schilling was born in Germany in 1835. After emigrating in 1842, he worked in New Jersey and Ohio before coming to Dubuque in 1857. He worked on many local buildings during the next thirty years.

Bernhard Schulte

Born in 1831 in Westphalia, Germany, Schulte learned stonecutting before coming to Dubuque in 1854. In 1857 he formed a partnership with Martin Wagner, another stonecutter. They worked together for a number of years and cut stone for several local projects including the tower of St. Raphael's.

OTHER CRAFTSMEN

Peter Klauer

Klauer was born in 1842 in Nassau, Germany. He came to Dubuque in 1855 where he learned the sheet metal trade. In 1870 he opened his own business manufacturing galvanized iron cornices, tin roofs and stoves. The firm he started has grown into the present Klauer Manufacturing Co.

J. W. Newburgh

Born in Ohio in 1840, Newburgh learned painting and frescoing in Detroit and Cleveland. He moved to Dubuque in 1862 and established his own business as a painter and creator of frescoes. By 1880 he employed fifteen men and worked on major projects throughout Iowa and as far away as Chicago and New York.

Acknowledgements

The idea for publishing **The Heritage of Dubuque; An Architectural View** originated at a meeting with Wayne A. Norman and Daniel Dittemore in October, 1974. The project, however, would not have been possible without the generous support of The First National Bank of Dubuque, whose Marketing Department was responsible for coordinating the bank's sponsorship of the book.

Many people cooperated to complete the book within a very short time period. Only seven months elapsed between the start of research and the time the manuscript went to the printer.

Extensive research assistance was provided by Helen Mercer, Director of the Dubuque County Historical Society, and William Painter, Reference Librarian at the Carnegie-Stout Public Library. Others who offered research material included John M. McDonald, Elsie Datisman, Rev. Norbert Barrett, Charles Geroux, Ted R. Ellsworth, Robert C. Wiederaenders, W. Frank McCaw, Wayne A. Norman, Jacqueline Merritt, Donald Conlon, Leo F. Frommelt, Alan B. Spensley, Margaret Zak, King Herr and Ruth Marshall. The Loras College Library and the Dubuque Planning and Zoning Commission office were additional sources of information about Dubuque's history and architecture.

Many of the photographs used in the book were taken by **Telegraph Herald** photographers. Altogether they made nearly 200 photographs available for use.

Besides producing the superb paintings and sketches that appear in the book, Galena artist Carl H. Johnson, Jr. played a major role in developing its design. Marilyn Kempthorne of Tel Graphics worked closely with the Publication Committee and was responsible for coordinating the printing schedule. Her specialized knowledge of typography and publishing was invaluable.

Although the entire Publication Committee reviewed the manuscript draft and offered many suggestions for its improvement, Robert Wiederaenders and Mary Alice Carroll deserve special mention for their outstanding editorial assistance. Valerie Cole typed the manuscript.

Photographs

Dubuque County Historical Society pp. 14, 15, 16, 17, 18, 19, 20, 21, 22, 23, 24, 25, 27, 28, 34, 47, 55, 94, 102, 112, 122, 127, 132

King Herr pp. 24, 25, 51, 55, 57, 78, 83, 97, 98, 115, 124, 127, 135, 137, 139, 141, 142, 144

John M. McDonald p. 27

Lawrence J. Sommer pp. 74, 136, 146, 148, 149, 150, 151, 152

Telegraph Herald pp. 17, 45, 47, 50, 65, 66, 74, 78, 80, 86, 90, 91, 94, 98, 99, 102, 103, 106, 107, 115, 117, 120, 127, 132, 134, 135, 136, 137, 138, 139, 140, 141

Wartburg Theological Seminary p. 26

The Doors

The Dubuque doors that appear on the chapter title pages can be found at the following locations:

p. 1	1108 Locust Street
p. 13	231 Bluff Street
p. 31	1455 Main Street
p. 67	1491 Main Street
p. 111	597 Loras Boulevard
p. 145	1389 Locust Street

The Author

Lawrence J. Sommer became interested in Dubuque architecture while working for the City Planning & Zoning Commission. Since 1968, much of his work has involved the integration of historic preservation activities into the town planning process. He graduated from Carleton College, Northfield, Minnesota, received an M.A. from the University of Minnesota and has also studied at Cornell University and in Europe. A native of northern Minnesota, he now lives in Duluth with his wife and daughter.

The Artist

Carl H. Johnson, Jr., his wife and four children, moved to Galena, Illinois from the Chicago area five years ago. His watercolors and etchings are shown at his private studio/gallery at 204 South Main Street in Galena and at the Fourth Street Artists in Dubuque. A native of the Chicago area, Mr. Johnson studied advertising design at the University of Illinois, in Champaign, where he received his B. F. A. in 1957. He worked as a commercial artist in the Chicago area with the S. Frederick Anderson Studios and later at his own free lance design studio in Hinsdale, Illinois.

Notes

DUBUQUE, THE KEY CITY

1. Dubuque **Express and Herald**, January 1, 1858.
2. Isadore Semper, **Pioneer Dubuque Through the Eyes of Visitors**, p. 14.
3. **Dubuque of Today, the Key City**, p. 9.

LOST HERITAGE
LANDMARKS THAT HAVE DISAPPEARED

1. Dubuque **Telegraph Herald**, March 9, 1932.
2. Dubuque **Weekly Times**, May 29, 1872.
3. **The History of Dubuque County,** 1880, p. 693.
4. Dubuque **Telegraph Herald,** August 17, 1947.
5. A. Munsell, **Dubuque Business Annual and Trade Review,** 1885, p. 15.
6. Dubuque **Telegraph Herald,** September 1, 1935.
7. Loren Horton, Early Architecture in Dubuque", **The Palimpsest,** September-October, 1974, p. 147.

A CENTURY OF DUBUQUE ARCHITECTURE
THE EARLY YEARS, 1830-1860

1. John Maass, **The Gingerbread Age,** p. 40.
2. Loren Horton, "Early Architecture in Dubuque", in **The Palimpsest,** September-October , 1974, p. 134.
3. **Dubuque Visitor,** May 11, 1836.
4. Horton, **op. cit.,** p. 135.
5. Dubuque **Miners Express,** 1852.
6. Horton, **op. cit.,** p. 136.
7. **ibid.**
8. Dubuque **Miners Express,** 1856.
9. Dubuque **Daily Times**, July 27, 1862.
10. **ibid.**
11. Horton, **op. cit.,** p. 137.
12. Marcus Whiffen, **American Architecture Since 1780, A Guide to the Styles,** p. 46 (from James Fennimore Cooper's **Home as Found**, 1838). For the sake of consistency Whiffen has been used throughout this book as the final source for naming the different architectural styles discussed.
13. **Dubuque City Directory**, 1860.
14. See "Lost Heritage" chapter.
15. He is sometimes credited as being the architect of the old Illinois State Capitol. Talbot Hamlin, in his book on Greek Revival architecture, lists Town and Davis as the architects and Rague as the construction supervisor (p. 310).
16. Whiffen, **op. cit.,** pp. 48 - 49.
17. **The History of Dubuque County,** 1880, p. 540.
18. Maass, **op. cit.,** p. 55.
19. Orson Squire Fowler, **The Octagon House**, p. 88.
20. See "Lost Heritage" chapter.
21. Maass, **op. cit.,** p. 97.
22. John Baule's book was published by and is available from the Dubuque County Historical Society.

A CENTURY OF DUBUQUE ARCHITECTURE
THE VICTORIAN YEARS, 1860-1890

1. John Maass, **The Gingerbread Age**, p. 15.
2. **Ibid.,** p. 14.

3. **Dubuque Business Annual and Trade Review,** 1886, p. 17.
4. **Dubuque City Directory,** 1885, p. 59.
5. **Descriptive Survey of Dubuque**, 1911, p. 23.
6. Mathias M. Hoffmann, **Centennial History of the Archdiocese of Dubuque,** p. 39.
7. **Centennial Brochure, St. Mary's Church,** p. 23.
8. **A Partial List of Windows Designed and Executed by Tiffany Studios,** p. 56.
9. Marcus Whiffen, **American Architecture Since 1780, A Guide to the Styles,** p. 111.
10. Maass, **op. cit.,** p. 120.
11. Dubuque **Express and Herald,** August 12, 1857. The article does not say who the other twelve men are.
12. Whiffen, **op. cit.**, p. 118.
13. **ibid.**
14. Roger Kennedy, **Minnesota Houses, an Architectural and Historical View,** p. 216.
15. **Portrait and Biographical Record of Dubuque, Jones and Clayton Counties,** p. 131.

A CENTURY OF DUBUQUE ARCHITECTURE THE LATER YEARS, 1890-1930

1. From National Register Nomination research data.
2. Dubuque **Daily Herald,** January 10, 1895.
3. **ibid.**
4. Dubuque **Daily Herald**, July 7 and 8, 1893.
5. **A Partial List of Windows Designed and Executed by Tiffany Studios,** p. 56. Tiffany's domestic windows were rarely signed, and the signature was sometimes omitted from their institutional and religious windows as well. When marked the signature was usually placed in the lower right corner and on the glass itself. The name varied:
   Tiffany Glass Company, New York
   Tiffany Glass and Decorating Company, New York
   Tiffany Studios, New York (1902)
   It is difficult to identify Tiffany glass by motifs or quality of stained glass. Other manufacturers made glass for use by Tiffany Studios, and flowers, trees, peacocks and other Tiffany motifs are also found in the work of other studios.
6. Mrs. Robert Steele and Dale Nederhoff, **A History of St. Luke's United Methodist Church, 1833 - 1975,** p. 8.
7. Dubuque Brewing and Malting Company, **Illustrated Guidebook.**
8. Dubuque **Telegraph Herald,** January 11, 1911.
9. Marcus Whiffen, **American Architecture Since 1780: A Guide to the Styles**, p. 147.
10. John Maass, **The Gingerbread Age**. p. 12.
11. Charles Geroux, **The History of Theaters and Related Theatrical Activity in Dubuque, Iowa, 1837 - 1877.**
12. Whiffen, **op. cit.,** p. 167.
13. Henry L. Williams and Ottalie K. Williams, **A Guide to Old American Houses, 1700 - 1900,** p. 65.
14. Whiffen, **op. cit.,** p. 221.
15. **ibid.,** p. 241.
16. **ibid.,** p. 246.
17. **ibid.,** p. 202.
18. Files of Dubuque Park Board.
19. **ibid.**
20. John Burchard and Albert Bush-Brown, **The Architecture of America, a Social and Cultural History,** p. 310.

Bibliography

The references cited include only works used during the research for this book. Many of the references contain extensive bibliographies that can be used by those persons who are interested in pursuing a given topic in more detail.

For convenience the bibliography is broken into three categories.

GENERAL ARCHITECTURAL HISTORY

Andrews, Wayne, **Architecture, Ambition and Americans,** New York, Harper's 1955.

Benjamin, Asher, **The American Builder's Companion,** New York, Dover Publications, 1969 (reprint of the 6th 1827 edition).

Burchard, John, and Albert Bush-Brown, **The Architecture of America, a Social and Cultural History,** Boston, Little, Brown & Company, 1961.

Carrott, Richard, "The Neo-Egyptian Style in American Architecture", in **Antiques**, October, 1966, pp. 482-488.

Downing, Andrew J., **The Architecture of Country Houses,** New York, Dover Publications, 1969 (reprint of the 1850 edition).

Drury, John, **Historic Midwest Houses,** New York, Bonanza Books, 1956.

Fitch, J. M., **American Building; the Forces that Shape It,** Boston, Houghton Mifflin, 1966.

Fletcher, Sir Banister, **A History of Architecture on the Comparative Method,** 17th edition, New York, Charles Scribner's Sons, 1961.

Fowler, Orson S., **The Octagon House, a Home for All,** New York, Dover Publications, 1973 (reprint of the 1853 edition entitled **A Home for All, or the Gravel Wall and the Octagon Mode of Building).**

Gillon, Edward V., and Clary Lancaster, **Victorian Houses; a Treasury of Lesser-Known Examples,** New York, Dover Publications, 1973.

Greiff, Constance M., **Lost America from the Mississippi to the Pacific,** Princeton, Pyne Press, 1974.

Hamlin, Talbot, **Greek Revival Architecture in America,** New York, Dover Publications, 1964 (reprint of 1944 Oxford University Press edition).

Kennedy, Roger, **Minnesota Houses; an Architectural and Historical View,** Minneapolis, Dillon Press, 1967.

Keyes, Margaret N., **Nineteenth Century Home Architecture of Iowa City,** Iowa City, University of Iowa Press, 1971.

Kimball, S. F., **A History of Architecture,** New York, 1946.

Maass, John, **The Gingerbread Age,** New York, Bramhall House, 1957.

McKee, Harley J., **Amateur's Guide to Terms Commonly Used in Describing Historic Buildings,** Rochester, New York, The Landmark Society, 1970.

Meyer, R. P., D. J. Smith and J. M. Dean, **Styles and Designs in Wisconsin Housing: A Guide to Styles,** Madison, University of Wisconsin Extension, 1974.

Mumford, Lewis, **Sticks and Stones, a Study of American Architecture and Civilization,** New York, Dover Publications, 1955 (reprint of the 1924 edition).

A Partial List of Windows Designed and Executed by Tiffany Studios, New York, Tiffany Studios, 1910, (reprinted 1972).

Perrin, Richard W. E., **The Architecture of Wisconsin,** Madison, The State Historical Society of Wisconsin, 1967.

Peterson, Charles E., "The Houses of French St. Louis", in **Missouri Historical Society Bulletin**, April, July, October, 1947 (reprinted in **The French in the Mississippi Valley).**

Van Rensselaer, Mariana Griswold, **Henry Hobson Richardson and His Works,** New York, Dover Publications, 1969.

Whiffen, Marcus, **American Architecture Since 1780: A Guide to the Styles,** Cambridge, MIT Press, 1969.

Williams, Henry L., and Ottalie K. Williams, **A Guide to Old American Houses, 1700 - 1900.** New York, A. S. Barnes, 1962.

HISTORIC PRESERVATION PLANNING

Bullock, Orin M., Jr., **The Restoration Manual,** Norwalk, Silvermine Publications, 1966.

Cullen, Gordon, **The Concise Townscape,** New York & London, Van Nostrand Reinhold Company, 1961

Feiss, Carl, Technical Director, **With Heritage So Rich,** New York, Random House, 1966 (Report of a Special Committee on Historic Preservation under the Auspices of the United States Conference of Mayors).

Halprin, Lawrence, **Cities,** Cambridge, MIT Press, 1972.

Kennet, Wayland, **Preservation**, London, Maurice Temple Smith, Ltd. 1972.

McKee, Harley J., Compiler, **Recording Historic Buildings**, Washington, D.C., U.S. Dept. of Interior, National Park Service, 1970.

Sommer, Lawrence, **The Heritage of Dubuque: a Preliminary Study of Historic Preservation Needs and Opportunities**, Dubuque, Planning and Zoning Commission, 1974.

Sommer, Lawrence, **Sample Legal Ordinances Relating to Historic Preservation,** Dubuque, Planning and Zoning Commission, 1974 (supplement to **The Heritage of Dubuque . . .**).

Stephen, George, **Remodeling Old Houses Without Destroying Their Character,** New York, Alfred A. Knopf, 1973.

Worskett, Roy, **The Character of Towns, An Approach to Conservation,** London, The Architectural Press, 1969.

Ziegler, Arthur P., **Historic Preservation in Inner City Areas, a Manual of Practice,** Pittsburgh, Allegheny Press, 1973.

DUBUQUE HISTORY AND ARCHITECTURE

Dubuque **Daily Times**

July 27, 1862 – article on shot tower
November 29, 1866 – article on General W. Lewis
January 1, 1880 – article on J. P. Farley House

Dubuque **Daily Herald**

November 30, 1890 – article on Dubuque County Court House
July 7 & 8, 1893 – article on Dubuque High School
January 14, 1894 – article on Mt. Carmel
January 10, 1895 – article on Dubuque High School
various dates – annual construction reviews

Dubuque **Express and Herald**

November 30, 1855 – annual construction review
March 18, 1857 – article on planned Methodist Church
August 12, 1857 – article on J. P. Farley
January 1 , 1858 – article on description of Dubuque

Dubuque **Daily Globe-Journal**

June 29, 1899 – article on F. Stout barn

Dubuque **Times Journal**

October 2, 1921 – article on old Dubuque landmarks
April 22, 1934 – article on first 2-story brick house

Dubuque **Telegraph Herald**

February 5, 1904 – article on sale of F. D. Stout house
November 11, 1911 – article on sale of F. D. Stout house
November 30, 1924 – article on model home at Kirkwood & Alta Vista
March 9, 1932 – article on old octagon house at 1672 Central
April 23, 1933 – article on Lewis-Adams house

August 6, 1933	– article on Langworthy brothers
February 4, 1934	– article on Ft. Rittenhouse
March 4, 1934	– article on S. Dixon house
March 8, 1934	– article on E. Porter house
April 15, 1934	– article on J. P. Farley house
April 22, 1934	– article on LeRoy Jackson house
May 27, 1934	– article on Tivoli Gardens
June 3, 1934	– article on J. Herancourt house
November 25, 1934	– article on S. Dixon house
September 1, 1935	– article on Turner Hall
July 11, 1937	– article on bluff homes
March 25, 1945	– article on J. Langworthy house
December 25, 1949	– article on shot tower
August 31, 1958	– centennial edition
February 11, 1959	– article on miscellaneous Dubuque houses
February 1, 1962	– article on Farley-Loetscher Company
April 5, 1964	– article on Alex. Simplot
September 24, 1972	– article on Dubuque City Hall
January –, 1974	– article on Thedinga house
February –, 1974	– article on Dubuque County Jail
May 11, 1975	– article on miscellaneous homes

Dubuque **Weekly Times**

May 29, 1872 – article on town clock collapse

Baule, John A., **The Ham House and the Life of Its Builder,** Dubuque, Dubuque County Historical Society, n.d.

Blumenson, John, "A Home for All - the Octagon in American Architecture", in **Historic Preservation,** July-September, 1973, pp. 30 - 35.

Callahan, Thomas J., **History of St. Raphael's Church Buildings,** Dubuque, Loras College, 1965, (unpublished thesis).

Datisman, Elsie, **Dubuque, Its History and Background,** Dubuque, Dubuque County Historical Society, 1969.

Descriptive Survey of Dubuque, Dubuque, Chamber of Commerce, 1911.

Dubuque and Its Neighborhood, Dubuque, Harger and Blish, 1897 **(Souvenir Gems of Dubuque).**

Dubuque Business Annual and Trade Review, 1886.

Dubuque City Directories

1856	1880	1915	1945
1857	1885	1921	1948
1858-59	1890	1925	
1860	1895	1929	
1865	1900	1934	
1870	1905	1937	
1875	1909	1941	

Dubuque County Gazeteer, Farmer's and Landowners' Directory, 1889.

"Dubuque Marks 125 Years of Progress," special issue of the Dubuque **Telegraph Herald,** August 31, 1958.

Dubuque of Today, the Key City, Dubuque, the Telegraph Printing Co., 1897.

Edwards Descriptive Gazetteer and Commercial Directory of the Mississippi River from St. Cloud to New Orleans, St. Louis, Edwards, Greenough & Deved, 1866.

Geroux, Charles L., **The History of Theaters and Related Theatrical Activity in Dubuque, Iowa 1837 - 1877,** Detroit, Wayne State University, Ph. D. dissertation, 1973.

Greenstein, Mrs. Saul, compiler, **The Flavor of Dubuque,** Dubuque, Women's Auxiliary of the Dubuque Symphony Orchestra, 1971.

Herrmann, Henry, **Land of Promise and Fulfillment,** East Dubuque, Tel Graphics, Inc. 1972 (for Dubuque County Historical Society and Dubuque Fraternity of Free Masons).

The History of Dubuque County, Chicago, Western Historical Company, 1880.

Hoffmann, M. M., **Antique Dubuque,** 1673 - 1833, Dubuque, 1933.

Hoffmann, M. M., **Centennial History of the Archdiocese of Dubuque,** Dubuque, Columbia College Press, 1938.

Hoffmann, M. M., "J. F. Rague, Pioneer Architect of Iowa", in **Annals of Iowa,** Vol. XIX, 1934, pp. 444-448.

Horton, Loren, "Early Architecture in Dubuque", in **The Palimpsest,** Vol. 55, No. 5 (September-October, 1974), Iowa City, The State Historical Society of Iowa, pp. 130-151.

Illustrated Guidebook to Dubuque Brewing and Malting Co., n.d.

Langworthy, L. H., **Dubuque, Its History, Mines, Indian Legends, etc.,** Dubuque, 1855.

"The Langworthys of Early Dubuque and Their Contributions to Local History", in **Iowa Journal of History and Politics,** 1910, pp. 315-464.

Munsel, A., **Dubuque Business Annual and Trade Review,** Dubuque, 1885.

Oldt, Franklin T., & P. J. Quigley, **History of Dubuque County, Iowa,** Chicago, Goodspeed Publishing Company, 1911.

O'Meara and Hills, **Catholic Churches and Institutions, O'Meara and Hills, Architects,** St. Louis, 1928.

One-Hundredth Anniversary, First Congregational Church, Dubuque, 1939.

Petersen, William J., "Dubuque - The Key City of Iowa", in **The Palimpsest,** Vol. XLV, No. 11 (November, 1964), Iowa City, The State Historical Society of Iowa.

Petersen, William J., **Steamboating on the Upper Mississippi,** Iowa City, State Historical Society of Iowa, 1968.

Portrait and Biographical Record of Dubuque, Jones and Clayton Counties, Chicago, Chapman Publishing Company, 1894.

Pratt, LeRoy G., **Discovering Historic Iowa,** Des Moines, Iowa, Dept. of Public Instruction, 1972.

Rider, Linda, ed., **Architecture in Dubuque,** Dubuque, Dubuque High School Author's Club, 1923.

Rosemary, Sr. O.S.F., **Historical Sketch of Mary of Angels Home,** Dubuque, 1932.

Semper, Isadore, **Pioneer Dubuque Through the Eyes of Visitors,** Dubuque, Loras College Press, 1954.

Shaffer, James, "Mississippi Mansion", in **The Iowan,** Fall, 1973, pp. 27-33.

Sigwarth, Rev. A., **The Story of St. Mary's in Pictures and Words,** Dubuque, St. Mary's Church, 1967.

Simplot, Alexander, **Souvenir of Dubuque, Iowa.** Dubuque, Alex. Simplot, publisher, 1891.

Steele, Mrs. Robert & Dale Nederhoff, **A History of St. Luke's United Methodist Church, 1833-1975,** Dubuque, 1975.

Sullivan, Roger A. & J. A. Swisher, "Dubuque Shot Tower", in **The Palimpsest,** December, 1949.

Tales of Dubuqueland, Dubuque, Souvenir Publishing Company, 1956.

The Treasures of St. Luke's Church, Dubuque, The Friends of St. Luke's Methodist Church, 1975.

Woodman, Betsy, **John Francis Rague, Mid-Nineteenth Century Revivalist Architect,** Iowa City, University of Iowa, M. A. Thesis, 1969, 339 pp.

Wulkow, Helen, **Dubuque in the Civil War Period,** Evanston, Northwestern University, M. A. Thesis, 1941, 105 pp.

INDEX

(D) building destroyed